Edexcel GCSE
Religious Studies

Unit 11
Islam

John Rudge
Diane Spradbery

A PEARSON COMPANY

Published by Pearson Education Limited, a company incorporated in England and Wales, having its registered office at Edinburgh Gate, Harlow, Essex, CM20 2JE. Registered company number: 872828

www.pearsonschoolsandfecolleges.co.uk

Edexcel is a registered trade mark of Edexcel Limited

Text © Pearson Education Limited 2010
First published 2010

14
10 9 8 7

British Library Cataloguing in Publication Data
A catalogue record for this book is available from the British Library.

ISBN 978 1 846904 26 4

Edited by Florence Production Limited, Stoodleigh, Devon
Typeset by HL Studios, Long Hanborough, Oxford
Produced by Florence Production Limited, Stoodleigh, Devon
Original illustrations © Pearson Education Limited 2010
Illustrated by HL Studios, Long Hanborough, Oxford
Cover design by Pearson Education Limited
Picture research by Zooid
Cover photo/illustration © Sami Sarkis Concepts/Alamy
Printed in Malaysia (CTP-PJB)

Acknowledgements
The authors and publisher would like to thank the following individuals and organisations for permission to reproduce copyright material:

Photos
Adrees Latif/Reuters/Corbis UK Ltd, p. 76; Alaa al-Marjani/Associated Press/Press Association Images, p. 67; Aleš Senožetnik/iStockphoto, p. 64; Alex Segre/Alamy, p. 43; Andy Crawford/dkimages.com, p. 32; ArkReligion.com/Alamy, p. 60; Associated Press/Press Association Images, p. 68; Athar Akram/ArkReligion.com/Alamy, p. 82; B. O'Kane/Alamy, p. 8; Charney Magri/arabianEye/Photolibrary Group, p. 36; Colin Underhill/Alamy, p. 46; Cubo Images/Robert Harding Picture Library, p. 52; David Levenson/Alamy, p. 45; dbimages/Alamy, p. 53; Diego Goldberg/Sigma/Corbis, p. 14; Digital Vision, p. 38; Elkie/Alamy, p. 73; Gaza Press/Rex Features, p. 93; Hasan Sarbakhshian/Associated Press/Press Association Images, p. 80; Ian Evans/Alamy, p. 51; Itsuo Inouye/Associated Press/Press Association Images, p. 48; Jamie Jones/Rex Features, p. 46; Jan Greune/LOOK-foto/Photolibrary Group, p. 22; Janine Wiedel Photolibrary/Alamy, p. 99; Janine Wiedel/Photofusion Picture Library, p. 108; Jim Craigmyle/Corbis p. 14; Jim West/Alamy, p. 106; JKimages/Alamy, p. 42; Khaled Desouki/AFP/Getty Images, pp. 78–79; Leonardo Diaz Romero/age fotostock/Photolibrary Group, p. 43; Luca Tettoni/Robert Harding Picture Library, p. 34; Marco Secchi/Alamy, p. 100; Mark Edward Smith/Tips Italia/Photolibrary Group, p. 36; Martin Meissner/Associated Press/Press Association Images, p. 44; MBI/Alamy, p. 63; Mohammad Hamza Mian/Alamy, p. 75; Muhammad Mahdi Karim/Photographers Direct/Micro2Macro, p. 16; Pascal Deloche/Godong/Corbis UK Ltd, p. 36; Paul Thuysbaert/GraphEast RM/Photolibrary Group, p. 111; Peter Titmuss/Alamy, p. 31; Photolibrary Group, p. 25; Press Association Images, p. 40; Qassem Zein/AFP/Getty Images, p. 71; Rex Features, pp. 18, 100; romain bayle/Alamy, p. 38; Rosemary Behan/Alamy, p. 4; Sally and Richard Greenhill/Alamy, p. 40; shcherbina galyna/Shutterstock, p. 69; Shutterstock, p. 18; StockTrek/Photodisc, pp. 12, 18; Stringer/India/Reuters/Corbis UK Ltd, p. 40; T. O'Keefe/Photodisc. 1999, p. 8; The British Library/Imagestate/Photolibrary Group, p. 36; Tracy Montana/Photodisc. 1996, p. 13; travelib/Alamy, p. 83; Vatikaki/Shutterstock, p. 38; World Religions Photo Library/Alamy, pp. 11, 95; World Religions Photo Library/Bridgeman Art Library, p. 10; Zooid Pictures, p. 102.

Text
The Holy Qur'an translation and commentary by A. Yusuf Ali. Used by permission of IPCI – Islamic Vision, Birmingham, UK.
P. 102: 2001 Census. Crown copyright 2003. P. 103: Charities Commission Survey of mosques in England and Wales. Crown copyright 2009.
Crown copyright material is reproduced with the permission of the Controller of HMSO.

With thanks to Tabassum Bachoo for reviewing, editing and providing guidance and information for this book, and for her help and guidance with other books in the series.

Websites
There are links to relevant websites in this book. In order to ensure that the links are up to date, that the links work, and that the sites are not inadvertently linked to sites that could be considered offensive, we have made the links available on the Heinemann website at www.pearsonhotlinks.co.uk. When you access the site, the express code is 4264P.

Disclaimer
This material has been published on behalf of Edexcel and offers high-quality support for the delivery of Edexcel qualifications.

This does not mean that the material is essential to achieve any Edexcel qualification, nor does it mean that it is the only suitable material available to support any Edexcel qualification. Edexcel material will not be used verbatim in setting any Edexcel examination or assessment. Any resource lists produced by Edexcel shall include this and other appropriate resources.

Copies of official specifications for all Edexcel qualifications may be found on the Edexcel website: www.edexcel.com

Contents

How to use this book...................................... iv

Section 1: Beliefs and values

Introduction 2
1.1 The nature and importance of belief in tawhid.. 4
1.2 The sin of shirk and why it is a major sin in Islam 6
1.3 The meaning and importance of belief in the creativity of Allah 8
1.4 The meaning and importance of belief in the mercy and compassion of Allah...................... 10
1.5 The meaning and importance of belief in Islamic teaching on the nature of humans as khalifah... 12
1.6 The meaning and importance of belief in Islamic teaching on al-Qadar and human freedom....... 14
1.7 The meaning and importance of belief in Islamic teaching on angels 16
1.8 The meaning and importance of belief in risalah... 18
1.9 The meaning and importance of belief in Islamic teaching on holy books................................ 20
1.10 The meaning and importance of belief in Islamic teaching on the revelation of the Qur'an to Muhammad 22
1.11 How belief in akhirah affects the lives of Muslims... 24
KnowZone.. 26

Section 2: Community and tradition

Introduction... 30
2.1 The meaning and importance of belief in Muhammad as the Seal of the Prophets 32
2.2 Why the Qur'an has supreme authority for Muslims 34
2.3 How and why Muslims show respect for the Qur'an 36
2.4 The nature and importance of the Shari'ah for Muslims 38
2.5 The importance and effects of the ummah...... 40
2.6 The main features of a mosque and the reasons for them 42
2.7 The role and importance of the imam in a mosque 44
2.8 The role and importance of the mosque for the local Muslim community 46
2.9 Reasons for the differences between Sunni and Shi'ah communities 48
2.10 The role and importance of groups and movements in British mosques 50
2.11 Different attitudes to Sufi forms of worship..... 52
KnowZone... 54

Section 3: Worship and celebration

Introduction 58
3.1 The meaning and significance of the Shahadah as a summary of Islamic belief 60
3.2 The practice and significance of salah 62
3.3 The practice and significance of zakah 64
3.4 The relationship of zakah to the ummah 66
3.5 The practice and significance of sawm during Ramadan 68
3.6 The reasons for and benefits of fasting............. 70
3.7 The meaning and significance of the celebration of Id-ul-Fitr... 72
3.8 The meaning and significance of the events of hajj in Makkah (1).. 74
3.8 The meaning and significance of the events of hajj in Makkah (2).. 76
3.9 The meaning and significance of the events of hajj at Arafat... 78
3.10 The meaning and significance of the events of hajj at Mina... 80
3.11 The meaning and significance of the celebration of Id-ul-Adha... 82
KnowZone.. 84

Section 4: Living the Muslim life

Introduction 88
4.1 The meaning and significance of the concepts of halal and haram 90
4.2 Islamic teaching on greater and lesser jihad and the effects of this teaching on a Muslim's life... 92
4.3 The meaning and significance of Islamic birth rituals 94
4.4 The meaning and significance of Islamic death rituals 96
4.5 The meaning and importance of Muslim attitudes to drugs and alcohol........................... 98
4.6 The implications of Muslim laws on dress when living in a western society 100
4.7 The implications of Muslim laws on food when living in a western society 102
4.8 The implications of Muslim laws on riba and gambling when living in a capitalist society ... 104
4.9 How and why some Muslims are involved in working for social and community cohesion .. 106
4.10 How Muslim organisations help to relieve poverty in the UK.. 108
4.11 The reasons why Muslim organisations work to relieve poverty and/or suffering in the UK 110
KnowZone.. 112
ExamZone.. 116
Glossary 122
Index 123

Welcome to this Edexcel GCSE in Religious Studies Resource

These resources are appropriate for GCSE Religious Studies students on both the modular GCSE course certified in 2012 and 2013, and the linear GCSE course certified from 2014. Each Student Book covers one unit of the specification which makes up a Short Course qualification. Any two units from separate modules of the specification make up a Full Course qualification. Packed with tips and activities, these books include lots of engaging features to enthuse students and provide the range of support needed to make teaching and learning a success for all ability levels.

Features in this book

In each section you will find the following features:

- **an introductory spread** which introduces the topics and gives the Edexcel key terms and learning outcomes for the whole section

- **topic spreads** containing the following features:

  - **Learning outcomes** for the topic

  - edexcel ⋮⋮⋮ key terms

    > **Specification key terms** – are emboldened in the text, and definitions can be found in the Glossary

  - **Activities** and **For discussion** panels provide stimulating tasks for the classroom and homework

  - a topic **Summary** which captures the main learning points

How to use this book

This book supports Unit 11 Islam. This unit can be combined with any unit from modules A, B, D.

This book is split into the four sections of the specification.

 A dedicated suite of revision resources. We've broken down the six stages of revision to ensure that you are prepared every step of the way.

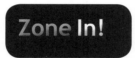 How to get into the perfect 'zone' for your revision.

 Tips and advice on how to plan your revision effectively.

 Revision activities and exam-style practice at the end of every section plus additional exam practice at the end of the book.

 Last-minute advice for just before the exam.

 An overview of what you will have to do in the exam, plus a chance to see what a real exam paper will look like.

 What do you do after your exam? This section contains information on how to get your results and answers to frequently asked questions on what to do next.

ResultsPlus

These features help you to understand how to improve, with guidance on answering exam-style questions, tips on how to remember important concepts and how to avoid common pitfalls.

There are three different types of ResultsPlus features throughout this book:

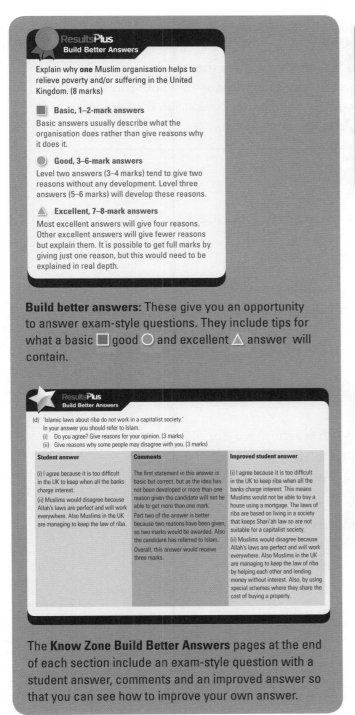

Build better answers: These give you an opportunity to answer exam-style questions. They include tips for what a basic ☐ good ◯ and excellent △ answer will contain.

The **Know Zone Build Better Answers** pages at the end of each section include an exam-style question with a student answer, comments and an improved answer so that you can see how to improve your own answer.

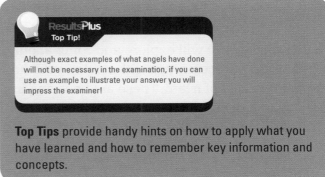

Top Tips provide handy hints on how to apply what you have learned and how to remember key information and concepts.

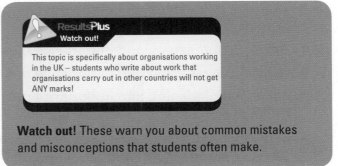

Watch out! These warn you about common mistakes and misconceptions that students often make.

Beliefs and values

Introduction

In this section you will explore and think about the beliefs and values that are important to Muslims. In particular, you will develop your understanding of what Muslims sometimes call the main beliefs of Islam. These are believing in God, His angels, His books, His messengers, the Day of Judgement, His decree of good and evil, and life after death.

Learning outcomes for this section

By the end of this section you should be able to:

- give definitions of the key terms and use them in answer to GCSE questions
- explain why believing in tawhid is important for Muslims
- explain why shirk is a major sin in Islam
- explain the meaning and importance of belief in the creativity of Allah
- explain the meaning and importance of belief in the mercy and compassion of Allah
- explain the meaning and importance of belief in Islamic teaching on the nature of humans as khalifah
- explain the meaning and importance of Islamic teaching on al-Qadar and human freedom
- explain the meaning and importance of Islamic teaching on angels
- explain the meaning and importance of belief in risalah
- explain the meaning and importance of belief in Islamic teaching on holy books other than the Qur'an
- explain the meaning and importance of belief in Islamic teaching on the revelation of the Qur'an to Muhammad
- explain how belief in akhirah affects the lives of Muslims
- express your own point of view about these beliefs using reasons and evidence
- show that you have thought about views that are different from your own.

edexcel ⋮⋮⋮ key terms

al-Qadar	ibadah	khalifah	risalah
creativity	iman	Muslim	shirk
din	Islam	Qur'an	tawhid

Look at the pictures of the men and women in the collage – which of these do you think are Muslims? Why? See if you agree with the person next to you. Can we be sure, from what they look like, whether a person is a Muslim?

Fascinating fact

Many Muslims become *hafiz*. This means that they can recite the whole of the Qur'an, the holy book of Islam, from memory. This is one of the ways in which Muslims show how important this book is for them.

In this section and the other three sections in this unit, you will find many references to the Qur'an.

1.1 The nature and importance of belief in tawhid

4

edexcel ▦ key terms

din – way of life (the belief and practice of Islam).

Islam – peace gained through submission to Allah.

Muslim – one who has submitted to Allah by accepting Islam.

Qur'an – that which is read or recited/the holy book of Islam.

tawhid – the oneness of Allah.

This inscription is on the Topkapi Palace in Istanbul. The Arabic words shown mean 'There is no god but Allah'. What do you think these words teach Muslims about tawhid?

Muslims believe in Allah. The word 'Allah' is the Arabic word for 'God'. **Tawhid** means believing in Allah, the one and only God. Muslims sometimes use the word 'unity' or 'oneness' to explain what they mean.

Unity is the idea that everything and everyone is united, or held together. For Muslims, it is Allah who holds everything in the universe together. No one else can do this, except Allah. Everything and every living creature depends on Him.

For Muslims, Allah is the One and Only One. He is also Number One. No one and nothing is like Him or can be compared with Him. He is Unique.

Activities

1 When we use the word 'one' it can have different meanings. Look at these phrases:
   - Number one
   - The first
   - The one and only
   - The best

   What ideas do they suggest?

2 Look up the words 'unique' and 'unity' in a dictionary. What ideas do these words give you to help explain what tawhid means?

For discussion

- Is believing that God is 'One' the most important belief about God?
- What other beliefs do people have about God?
- Do you agree with any of these beliefs? Why or why not?

Why is this belief important for Muslims?

Believing in the unity of Allah, that Allah is One, that Allah is Unique, that nothing can be compared with Allah, is the foundation of **Islam**. Everything else that Muslims believe or do stems from this belief. It is important to Muslims for the following reasons:

- It is taught in the **Qur'an**, which Muslims believe to be the word of Allah.

- It helps Muslims make sense out of life. For many people life is very confusing. For Muslims, believing that Allah is Unique and holds everything together helps them to make sense of their lives, whatever happens to them. It helps to give them a sense of purpose and direction. It helps them to see how everything in life fits together.

- It helps Muslims to think of Allah, and not themselves, as the centre, the focal point of life.

- It helps Muslims to follow the teaching and example of the Prophet Muhammad. The focal point of the Prophet's life was Allah. He showed how to live a full and faithful life because his life was focused on Allah.

Activities

3 What do you think it means for a Muslim to live a life focused on Allah?

4 Choose two of the following situations and think about what a Muslim's reaction might be to them.

Situation	What might a Muslim do?
Getting an A* in an exam	
A friend getting into trouble	
Someone making fun of the clothes you wear	

How do Muslims try to show their belief in the oneness of Allah?

Muslims believe that because Allah is at the centre of everything and because He is Unique, every part of their lives – and of the religion of Islam – should also focus on this centre, this unity of Allah, this uniqueness. How do Muslims show this in their lives? Here are some examples:

- They recognise that no one and nothing else is worth worshipping apart from Allah.
- All living creatures must be treated with respect, because all life comes from Allah and belongs to Allah.
- The Muslim community should also be one, united and held together by their belief in Allah because Allah is One.
- When Muslims believe in Allah, and when they keep Allah at the centre of everything they do, they are being true to their **din**.

Activities

Challenge

5 Using books or the Internet, or by talking to a Muslim, see if you can find out about other examples where the unity and oneness of Allah is shown by Muslims.

6 Not everyone in the world believes that God is the 'unique centre of life'. What other beliefs do people hold about the meaning and purpose of life, about what life is for? Try to pick out some reasons why they hold these beliefs. Do you agree with them? Which of these reasons do you think is the strongest?

Summary

For Muslims, belief in tawhid is the foundation of their faith. They believe that Allah is at the centre of everything and nothing can be compared to Him.

1.2 The sin of shirk and why it is a major sin in Islam

Learning outcomes

By the end of this lesson, you should be able to:

- state what Muslims believe about shirk
- give your own opinion, with a reason, about the importance of this belief
- explain why this belief is important for Muslims
- evaluate different points of view about this belief, with reasons.

edexcel ⠿ key terms

ibadah – All acts of worship/any permissible action performed to obey Allah.

shirk – The sin of regarding anything as an equal or partner of Allah.

Activities

2 Look at four passages from the Qur'an (5:76; 16:51; 23:91; 112:1–4). What do these passages say about shirk?

Activities

1 There are many bad things people can do; here are some examples:
- harming another person
- telling a lie
- cheating on a friend
- being cruel to animals
- losing their temper
- stealing
- killing a person.

Would you add anything else to the list? Which of these things do you think is the worst? Why? Create a chart with the worst at the top.

What is shirk?

The worst thing a Muslim can do is to put anyone or anything on the same level as Allah, to worship anyone or anything else but Allah. Many Muslims believe it is a sin that can never be forgiven. If a person does this, they stop being a Muslim. So Muslims take this very seriously. They are very careful to avoid it.

Shirk means 'association'. It is the idea of associating anyone or anything with Allah, or thinking that anyone or anything can be equal to Allah, or like Allah, or can be worshipped. This is because worship can only be given to Allah, and to Allah alone. Shirk is sometimes called 'idolatry', which means worshipping an idol or something that is not real. For Muslims, only Allah is real.

Why is shirk such a major sin?

The sin of shirk is the only sin that will not be forgiven. The Qur'an states 'Allah forgives not that partners should be set up with Him...' (Surah 4:48).

1 Belief in tawhid, the oneness of Allah, is the most basic principle of Islam. Allah is divine and not part of the material world so nothing is as great as Him and nothing can be associated with Him. This was the message that Muhammad gave to the people of Makkah when he threw the idols out of the Ka'bah. To make anyone or anything equal with Allah, the sin of shirk, goes against that principle. This is why Muslims disagree with Christians about the divinity of the prophet Isa (Jesus).

2 Shirk breaks the commitment that Muslims make when they recite the Shahadah, 'There is no God but Allah'.

3 For Muslims, Islam is the only true and pure religion – the sin of shirk takes away that purity by equating Allah with other things.

4 Worship of Allah defines the way a Muslim lives on Earth. Every action, whether small or large, must glorify Allah. These acts are called **ibadah** from the word meaning a 'slave' or 'servant'. Nothing must get in the way of Allah's rightful place as the first and most important influence in a Muslim's life. Tawhid is the basis of everything a Muslim does and by avoiding shirk a Muslim is emphasising the importance of Allah in their life.

How do Muslims avoid shirk?

Worship is not just about what people do in a religious building, or when they are praying. It refers to anything or anybody to whom we give worth or regard as important or worthwhile. In this sense, it is possible to worship or to give most importance to many different things in life.

One way in which Muslims avoid shirk is by making sure that they concentrate only on Allah when they pray. That is why there are never any pictures of people in the mosque, including no pictures of the Prophet. This is meant to keep them from being distracted. It helps them to think only about Allah.

Most Muslims find no real difficulty in believing that there is no God but Allah, or in avoiding the worship of other gods or idols. What they may find more difficult is making sure nobody and nothing ever takes the central place of Allah in their lives. That is the struggle (jihad) in which they are engaged throughout their lives.

Activities

3 With a partner, make a list of things (or people) that could take the place of Allah in the everyday life of a Muslim. The pictures on this page will give you some ideas. How could they become 'idols'?

Which of these, for a Muslim, do you think would be the most dangerous?

4 Find out what happened when the Prophet Muhammad cleared the idols out of the Ka'bah. Why did he do this?

For discussion

- Why do you think some people suggest that selfishness, or self-centredness, is the most dangerous form of shirk? Why is self-centredness 'the opposite of tawhid'?

- Many Muslims refer to the struggle (jihad) within themselves against self-centredness as the 'greater jihad' (see pages 92–93). Why do you think this is seen as the most difficult form of idolatry to avoid?

Activities

5 Muslim teaching about shirk contains some important insights and warnings for everyone, not just for Muslims. What lessons can a non-Muslim learn from this teaching of Islam?

Summary

Shirk is a major sin in Islam. It means to worship or regard anything as equal to or more important than Allah and is the thing that all Muslims should avoid doing.

1.3 The meaning and importance of belief in the creativity of Allah

Learning outcomes

By the end of this lesson, you should be able to:

- state what Muslims mean by 'the creativity of Allah'
- give your own opinion, with a reason, about this belief
- explain why this belief is important for Muslims
- evaluate different points of view about this belief, with reasons.

edexcel ⠿ key terms

creativity – The action of creating the universe by Allah.

iman – Faith in Allah.

Activities

1 What do you think it is about a dome that reminds Muslims of the universe? Share ideas with a partner.

Many Muslims think of the dome of a mosque as representing the universe.

Muslims believe in the **creativity** of Allah and that Allah created the universe. This follows from the belief that Allah is One and that there is nothing and no one that can compare with Allah. The 'idea' of the universe comes from Allah. He is also the one who makes the universe happen, who creates it and keeps it going. More importantly for human beings, Allah is the one who creates life on the earth, with all its many varied forms, all the different creatures who share the earth with us and all the laws that control the way we live. All life comes from Allah.

Muslims do not agree with the idea that the universe, and the earth, are just here by chance. All the time scientists are discovering how the world works. For Muslims, this means that they are discovering new things about the creativity of Allah. But not everyone agrees that these discoveries show that Allah is the Creator.

In the end, no one can be certain that the evidence proves that Allah did, or did not, create the universe. For Muslims, this is a matter of faith (**iman**). This means they trust that Allah created the universe, and they try to live their lives in such a way that they show that this is their belief. Most Muslims will base their belief not on any proof from science, but on the teaching of the Qur'an, although many believe that science supports the Qur'anic teachings.

It means that the universe and all human life are under the control of Allah. It is Allah who determines what will happen, not human beings. It is Allah who has the power to control everything. The power of Allah as the Creator is so much greater than that of His creation.

Why is the belief in the creativity of Allah important for Muslims?

It means that Muslims are able to recognise that the order and beauty of life come from Allah. They are able to see the world as a place where Allah is in control and therefore they have nothing to fear from it, even if they do not always understand everything about it. There is nothing beyond the control of Allah.

It means that all life belongs to Allah. Because Allah is the source of life, life itself is precious and is given to human beings as a gift. Indeed life is the most precious gift of all. Human beings must therefore treat all life with care.

Although scientists have discovered many things about how the universe works, human knowledge is limited and can never understand all the wishes and purposes of Allah. Human beings are part of the creation of Allah and are therefore limited in their view of things, especially as their lives and their thoughts are confined to the world of time and space. Allah, whose power is not limited, is not confined to the world of time and space.

Activities

2 Look at these words from the Qur'an. What do they teach about Allah the Creator?

> *'Praise be to Allah, the Cherisher and Sustainer of the Worlds.'* (Surah 1:2)
>
> *'… Nor shall they compass anything of His knowledge except as He wills…'* (Surah 2:255)

Activities

3 Share ideas about the word 'evidence'. What different types of evidence can you think of – mathematical proof, scientific discoveries, what people say and so on? What is the difference between them?

4 How do you think a Muslim would respond to someone who said that:
- all the evidence points to the conclusion that life is an accident of nature
- beauty is only in the eye of the beholder
- the basis of life is random selection
- the universe originated in a vast explosion of matter that eventually settled, after billions of years, into the universe as it is today
- this process will go on for ever.

 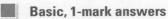

ResultsPlus
Build Better Answers

Do you think Allah created the universe?
Give **two** reasons for your point of view. (4 marks)

■ **Basic, 1-mark answers**
These answers would give an opinion but supported by one simple reason only.

● **Good, 2–3-mark answers**
Good answers will support their opinion with one developed and one simple reason.

▲ **Excellent, 4-mark answers**
Excellent answers will support their opinion with two developed reasons.

Summary

Muslims believe that Allah created the universe and everything in it. This affects how they view the world and how they live their lives.

1.4 The meaning and importance of belief in the Mercy and Compassion of Allah

Learning outcomes

By the end of this lesson, you should be able to:

● state what Muslims mean by the mercy and compassion of Allah

● give your own opinion, with a reason, about this belief

● explain why this belief is important for Muslims

● evaluate different points of view about this belief, with reasons.

In fact, almost every surah (chapter) in the Qur'an begins with the words of the bismillah (see page 34) shown in the picture which can be translated as: '*In the name of Allah, Most Compassionate, Most Merciful*'. So these two names are clearly very important for Muslims.

Activities

1 Think of an occasion when someone has been kind to you. What happened and how did it make you feel?

Famous people (especially in history) are sometimes given names to describe what they are like, such as Alfred the Great and Ivan the Terrible. The name tells you something about the person's character.

The bismillah.

Muslims are very careful not to try to describe Allah, because Allah is so great that He cannot be described. However, the Qur'an helps them to understand what Allah is like because it uses many different names to tell people about the character of Allah. In fact, there are 99 of these names in the Qur'an, and they all say something about what Muslims believe Allah is like. Two that appear very often are the names 'Compassionate' and 'Merciful'.

When Muslims say that Allah is 'the Compassionate' and 'the Merciful', they mean that Allah is kind in the way He deals with people:

● Allah forgives them
● Allah loves them
● Allah supports them
● Allah cares for them.

Muslims believe that Allah is always kind, whatever happens to them in life. Sometimes they get into difficulties and sometimes they suffer pain, but they still try to trust in Allah's kindness even if they do not understand why they are suffering. When they are going through hard times, they trust that they will never walk alone.

Activities

2 Can you think of other words that mean the same thing as compassionate and merciful? Look up the meaning of the word 'sympathetic'. What does it mean if a friend is sympathetic to you?

3 Some people find it really difficult to believe that God is kind. Why do they find this difficult? Why do you think some people do not believe in God because of this?

Why is the belief in the Compassion and Mercy of Allah important for Muslims?

- **Without this belief, Muslims would feel hopeless.** This is because they often fail to live as Allah requires. If Allah dealt with them as they deserve, they believe they would be punished for the wrongs they have done. But instead, Allah is Merciful when they sincerely repent and ask for His forgiveness, and He treats them with compassion, because of their weaknesses.

- Muslims believe that Allah is also their judge, especially when their lives end and they have to account for the way they have lived. If Allah was not Merciful and Compassionate, no one would survive the judgements of Allah who is always fair and just in His dealings with people. **This belief gives Muslims courage that it is worth striving to live a good life.**

- The Mercy and Compassion of Allah help Muslims to improve the quality of their lives because **it strengthens their love for Allah** and their devotion to Him. If Allah were merciless and cruel, they would only regard Him with fear and terror. But since He is Kind and Forgiving, their love for Him grows.

A Muslim using a tasbih (prayer beads) to meditate on the ninety-nine names of Allah.

- Muslims must also remember that Allah's qualities of Compassion and Mercy are not the only qualities mentioned in the Qur'an. There are also qualities that emphasise His Power, Justice and Wisdom. Muslims must not think that Allah will always deal gently with them, whatever they do. However, **Allah will always be fair with them, and never lead them astray.**

Activities

4   You should start to become familiar with the 'Ninety-nine beautiful names of Allah'. You can find the ninety-nine names on the Internet. Go to www.pearsonhotlinks.co.uk (express code 4264P) and click on the appropriate link. Put the word 'compassion' at one end of a line and 'punishment' at the other end. How many names would you place towards the 'compassion' end, and how many towards the 'punishment' end? Names that emphasise 'power' and 'wisdom' can be placed towards the middle. Do more names emphasise the gentle qualities or the harsher qualities?

Are mercy and compassion the most important qualities of Allah?

A Muslim will, of course, emphasise that *all* the names of Allah are important. No quality is more important than any other. That is why, when Muslims use the tasbih, they meditate on all the qualities of Allah. They try, as far as they can, to make these qualities part of their own lives.

Activities

Challenge

5   Can you find out about some of the occasions on which Muslims use the words of the bismillah? What do these occasions tell you about their importance?

Summary

The Muslim belief that Allah is Compassionate and Merciful is important for Muslims because it shows them that Allah will treat them kindly and it is worth striving to live a good life.

11

1.5 The meaning and importance of belief in Islamic teaching on the nature of humans as khalifah

Learning outcomes

By the end of this lesson, you should be able to:

- state what Muslims mean by the word 'khalifah'
- give your own opinion, with a reason, about this belief
- explain why this belief is important for Muslims
- evaluate different points of view about this belief.

Humans as khalifah

The idea of 'minding the world' and 'taking care of the Earth' is very important for Muslims. It affects the way they look at the world around them and reminds them that:

- the world belongs to Allah
- Allah gives people (and especially Muslims) responsibility for taking care of the world for His pleasure
- they have a duty to look after it and make sure it is used properly
- they must not allow it to be misused
- they must give Allah an account of what they have done to make Allah's world a better place in which to live.

The word Muslims use to describe this responsibility for the world is **khalifah**. It means 'minder' or 'steward' or 'deputy'. All human beings are the khalifahs of Allah.

Who do you think the Earth belongs to? Give two reasons for your view.

edexcel ::: key terms

khalifah – Custodian or steward of the world for Allah.

Activities

1 Imagine that you are the owner of a sweet shop. You are going away on holiday and have asked someone else to look after the shop while you are away. Write a list of what you would expect this person to do.

2 Now imagine that you are the person who has been asked to look after the shop. Write a list of what you would do while the shop owner is away. Then write an explanation for why you would do this. What, if anything, do you owe to the shop owner?

3 Apart from believing in Allah, do you think there are other good reasons for looking after the world? What reasons would you give? Does it matter whether humans care for the world? Do you think it makes a difference to the way people look after the world if they believe in Allah?

One reason why Muslims believe they are given this responsibility is because of one of the teachings in the Qur'an. In this teaching, the first human being, according to Islam, was Adam. Allah appointed Adam as the first khalifah. He was to pass on this responsibility to all people who came after him.

'Behold, your Lord said to the angels: "I will create a vicegerent on earth…"' (Surah 2:30)

Here are some other possible meanings of the word 'khalifah':

Regent Manager AGENT Representative Steward

Dealing with rubbish is becoming a problem in the UK.

Activities

4 What do you think is the main characteristic of all these roles? What is the most important part of these roles?

Why is this important to Muslims?

Islamic belief in people as khalifahs of Allah is important for a number of reasons:

- It helps to make clear the relationship, according to Islam, between humans and Allah. There are two sides to this relationship. On the one side, humans are second only to Allah in the order of creation. On the other side, human beings are clearly not 'masters of the universe'. That role belongs to Allah alone.

- People have to use their reason and skills to decide how they should care for the Earth. The best way to do this is not always obvious. But the starting point for human reason is to accept that the Earth belongs to Allah, not to human beings.

- According to Islam, Allah has given humans authority over all other living creatures. So humans stand out from the rest of creation. Only they have this responsibility for the Earth. Allah has given them authority and put them in charge.

- Humans are answerable to Allah on the Day of Judgement for their stewardship. They are accountable to Allah. Even though they may try to avoid any sense of responsibility during their own lifetime, saying that the problems are too great to solve or arguing that the Earth is simply here for human beings to enjoy or exploit, they must eventually answer to Allah for their deeds (or the lack of them).

Activities

5 One of the biggest challenges for humans is to know how best to show their responsibility for the Earth. Which of the following three attitudes do you think shows the greatest sense of responsibility? (You might be able to think of actual examples of these attitudes today.)

- Leave the Earth to look after itself because nature will always take its own course.
- Intervene only when nature seems to be going astray.
- Manage and control the Earth and its resources carefully for the benefit of humans.

6 Do you think that humans are any different from other creatures? Why? Why not?

7 Do humans have any responsibility for the future of the Earth? What reasons would you give for your answer? What reasons might someone else, who disagrees with you, give?

Summary

Muslims believe that Allah made Adam the first khalifah of the Earth, which means that he was asked to look after it. Muslims also believe that Adam passed this on to all humans so that every person should act as a khalifah of the Earth. This is important to Muslims because it clarifies their relationship with Allah and the world.

1.6 The meaning and importance of belief in Islamic teaching on al-Qadar and human freedom

Learning outcomes

By the end of this lesson, you should be able to:

- state what Muslims mean by al-Qadar and human freedom
- give your own opinion, with a reason, about this belief
- explain why this belief is important for Muslims
- evaluate different points of view about this belief, with reasons.

Activities

1 With a partner discuss how far people in the pictures (a) had a choice about their lives and (b) have the freedom to change their situations.

Meaning and importance of al-Qadar

Belief in **al-Qadar** is very important for Muslims. Muslims believe that everything that happens to us in life is because Allah is in control and knows what will happen in the future. That means both 'good' and 'bad' things. Muslims should accept that Allah decides what is best for them.

Al-Qadar is important to Muslims because:

- it is stated in the Qur'an
- it was taught by the Prophet Muhammad
- submitting to the will of Allah is at the heart of being a Muslim
- it helps Muslims make sense of the world – knowing that Allah has knowledge of everything and is in control of all events must mean that everything happens for a reason.

edexcel ⠿ key terms

al-Qadar – Allah's control of future events.

Who is in control of people's lives?

Activities

2 Make a list of five situations in which you think you are completely free to do whatever you want, and five situations in which you think you have no choice at all.

3 When Muslims plan anything in their lives, like a holiday, they often say 'insh'Allah', which means 'if Allah wishes'. Why do you think they say this? What difference could it make to their plans?

4 Can you think of other occasions in life when a Muslim might say 'if Allah wishes'?

5 When something dreadful happens, a Muslim will sometimes say 'it is the will of Allah'. Explain how this might help them to get through the bad times in life.

6 Do you think our lives are decided for us before we are born? Give two reasons to support your point of view.

Free will

Muslims believe that everything in this world and in our lives is under the control of Allah because Allah is all-powerful – there are no limits or restrictions on what He can do. At the same time, Allah has given all His human creatures free will, which means that they are free to choose whether to act in a good or evil way. This is one thing that makes humans different from animals.

On Judgement Day, Muslims believe they will be judged by Allah on how they have lived their lives. Without free will, the judgement would be unfair – it would not be just to reward or punish people if they were simply robots, unable to think for themselves. This means, therefore, that humans are responsible for all their actions – they must give an answer to Allah on the Day of Judgement for what they have done, good or evil – and because Allah knows all, Allah cannot be deceived.

Watch out!

Be careful not to confuse the terms 'al-Qadar' and 'free will'.

Muslims generally do not try to resolve the apparent conflict between al-Qadar and free will. However, they do believe that Allah knows best, and that Allah will always be fair.

Build Better Answers

'Whatever happens to you in life is just a matter of luck.'
In your answer you should refer to Islam.
(i) Do you agree? Give reasons for your opinion. (3 marks)
(ii) Give reasons why some people may disagree with you. (3 marks)

Both parts of this question will be marked in the same way.

■ **Basic, 1-mark answers**

These answers will give one basic reason. Be aware of the difference between saying what you think and giving reasons why you think it.

● **Good, 2-mark answers**

These will either give two brief reasons or one developed reason. 'Developed' means you say something extra to explain your reason.

▲ **Excellent, 3-mark answers**

Answers that get full marks will either give three brief reasons or two developed reasons. They could also give one reason, but this would need to be fully developed.

Summary

The belief in al-Qadar is central to being a Muslim. It means that Allah knows everything that has happened and everything that will happen for all eternity – nothing occurs without Allah's knowledge.

1.7 The meaning and importance of belief in Islamic teaching on angels

Learning outcomes

By the end of this lesson, you should be able to:

- outline what Muslims believe about angels
- give your own opinion, with a reason, about this belief
- explain why this belief is important for Muslims
- evaluate different points of view about this belief, with reasons.

Activities

1   In pairs make a list of the ways you communicate with people. Which of these ways do you think is the most effective? Which way would be best if you could not see the person? Give reasons for your answer.

At the end of prayers, Muslims turn to the right and the left and say, 'Peace and the mercy of Allah be on you.' Who are they saying this to?

Angels in Islam

Angels are referred to quite often in the Qur'an. The main teachings about them are:

- they are made from light
- they were created to carry out the exact instructions of Allah
- they have no free will so are counted as lower in importance than humans
- the number of them is limitless
- they are invisible, but on special occasions they may appear in human form.

Some angels are mentioned by name in the Qur'an. Muslims believe these angels are important because of what they do and the events with which they are associated. Here are some of them:

- Jibril, who brought the words of the Qur'an to the Prophet Muhammad
- Izra'il, the angel of death
- Mika'il, the guardian of places of worship
- Israfil, the herald of the day of resurrection
- Munkar and Nakir, who question the dead in their graves.

Many Muslims believe that throughout their lives they are accompanied by two angels who sit on their shoulders, one on their right and the other on their left. One records the good deeds that a person does during their lifetime, and the other records the evil deeds. These records are kept faithfully until the Day of Judgement.

Muslims use the end of prayer to ask that the blessings of Allah may be given to all the worshippers on each side of them – in other words, to their fellow Muslims in the mosque. But not only in the mosque, also to all Muslims everywhere and, in turn, to the whole human creation of Allah. Many Muslims also believe this is asking the blessing of Allah upon their two angels.

Why are angels important?

Angels are a vital part of communicating a person's good and bad thoughts and deeds back to Allah on the Day of Judgement.

Muslims believe that angels communicate the exact, uncorrupted message of Allah to human beings, particularly when that message is extremely important. You will learn more about this on pages 22–23 (section 1.10).

The Qur'an mentions other important tasks which certain angels carry out – such as guarding places of worship.

Many Muslims believe that angels (as well as Allah Himself) protect them when they pray.

For discussion

Muslims do not try to imagine what angels look like, and they think it is completely wrong to draw pictures of angels. Why do Muslims think it is wrong to do this?

ResultsPlus
Top Tip!

Although exact examples of what angels have done will not be necessary in the examination, if you can use an example to illustrate your answer you will impress the examiner!

Activities

2   Write a paragraph explaining why angels are important in Islam.

3   Do you believe in angels? Give reasons for your answer.

Summary

Muslims believe that angels are made by Allah to serve Him. They are important because they communicate messages to humans and keep track of the good and bad thoughts and actions of people during their lives.

1.8 The meaning and importance of belief in risalah

Learning outcomes

By the end of this lesson, you should be able to:

- outline what Muslims believe about risalah
- give your own opinion, with a reason, about this belief
- explain why this belief is important for Muslims
- evaluate different points of view about this belief, with reasons.

Activities

1 If you wanted someone to pass on a message, what sort of person would you choose? What qualities would you look for?

2 Think of the way radio messages are sent today.

- There has to be a producer, who decides what the message is and transmits it.
- There have to be waves that carry the message.
- There has to be a receiver and broadcaster.

Can you suggest, for Muslims, who these three might represent for the message of Islam?

The prophets

Muslims believe that Allah chooses His messengers. These messengers are called prophets. Allah chose His messengers because they brought His message accurately, they taught people how to follow the message and they lived their own lives according to the message. This is known as **risalah**.

Most Muslims believe that Allah sent 124,000 messengers and the Qur'an mentions some of them by name. Muslims believe that all these messengers are important, because they brought the guidance of Allah to different nations at various times, but their message was the same. It was the message of Islam.

edexcel ::: key terms

risalah – Muslim beliefs about the prophets of Allah.

Radio broadcasting: an example of one of the ways a message can be transmitted.

Build Better Answers

'People can never be sure that a message is really from God.'

In your answer you should refer to Islam.

(i) Do you agree? Give reasons for your opinion. (3 marks)

(ii) Give reasons why some people may disagree with you. (3 marks)

Both parts of this question will be marked in the same way.

 Basic, 1-mark answers

These answers will give one basic reason. Be aware of the difference between saying what you think and giving reasons why you think it.

● **Good, 2-mark answers**

These will either give two brief reasons or one developed reason. 'Developed' means you say something extra to explain your reason.

 Excellent, 3-mark answers

Answers that get full marks will either give three brief reasons or two developed reasons. They could also give one reason, but this would need to be fully developed.

Here are some of the important messengers or prophets of Allah:

● The first prophet, Adam, was also the ancestor of the whole human race.

● Another important prophet was Ibrahim – you can read about him in Surah 2 in the Qur'an. This is the same prophet that Jewish and Christian people call Abraham.

● Musa (Moses) was the prophet who brought the message of Islam to the Hebrew and Jewish people.

● Isa was the prophet known as Jesus in the Bible.

Muslims believe that these prophets all brought the same message of Allah. The message of Allah has not changed from the beginning. The Qur'an sometimes refers to this message as 'guidance'.

Why is the belief in risalah important?

1 Prophets brought the guidance of Allah to different nations at different times showing that the message was from the beginning.

2 All prophets brought the same message showing that Allah is unchanging.

3 All prophets brought the same message of Islam showing that Islam is the true religion.

4 All prophets prepared the way for the final prophet, Muhammad.

Activities

3 What do you think people mean by 'guidance'? Is it the same as 'orders', 'rules', 'instructions', 'advice' or 'ideas'? What makes guidance different from the others? What does this tell us about how Muslims think of Allah?

4 Find out what the Qur'an says about prophet Ibrahim (see Surah 2:127–9; 6:75–83; 14:35–41; 37:100–11).

5 How does Ibrahim help to bring the three religions of Judaism, Christianity and Islam closer together?

6 Can you find one story in the Qur'an that is similar to a story in the Jewish Torah and the Christian Bible? What does this story teach about God?

Summary

Muslims believe that Allah has chosen many prophets to bring the message of Islam to people. This belief is known as risalah.

1.9 The meaning and importance of belief in Islamic teaching on holy books other than the Qur'an

Learning outcomes

By the end of this lesson, you should be able to:

● outline Islamic teaching on holy books other than the Qur'an

● give your own opinion, with a reason, about this belief

● explain why this belief is important for Muslims

● evaluate different points of view about this belief, with reasons.

Activities

1 Choose two or three people to go outside the room. One person in the room tells a short story to the class. Choose a member of the class to repeat the story and ask one of the students to come in and listen. Then that student repeats the story to the next person who comes in and so on. When everyone is back inside the last person repeats the story and the rest of the class judge how accurate it is when compared with the original.

The tawrat – this was given by Allah to the prophet Musa (Moses). Many people equate this to the Jewish Torah or the five Books of Moses from the Christian Bible.

The zabur – this was a collection of hymns and songs which Muslims believe was used for worship in Soloman's temple in Jerusalem. They believe that many of these were written by Dawud (David). Some scholars equate this back to the Biblical book of Psalms.

The injil – this was the revelation received by Isa (Jesus). Some scholars equate this to the four Gospels of the Christian Bible, although this is debated.

The tawrat, zabur and injil

Muslims believe that throughout history Allah has sent His message to people on Earth through prophets such as Musa and Isa who were sent to particular nations and peoples at a particular time. Some of these prophets received direct revelation from Allah, which were recorded in different holy books. These books are all referred to in the Qur'an.

Muslims believe that originally these books all contained the same message from Allah. However, many were written hundreds or thousands of years after they were revealed and have repeatedly been translated and amended over time so that the message given by Allah to His prophets was changed. In other words, Allah's message in these books has been distorted so that the original meaning has been lost.

Muslims believe that today these books contain many errors – for example, they believe that the Christian Gospels have been changed by people to say that Isa was crucified and arose from the dead. Instead, Muslims believe that Isa did not die but was ascended to Heaven by Allah.

Therefore, although these books contain some truth, they have become distorted so that Muslims do not use them as a guide for living because they are unreliable. The only holy book that contains the total and complete truth is the Qur'an because of the way it was revealed to Muhammad and because it has not been changed (see pages 22–23).

The importance of this belief

Islamic teachings on holy books other than the Qur'an are important because:

- they demonstrate that Allah cares for people because Allah revealed His message directly to people over time

- they show that only the Qur'an contains the whole truth – therefore only Islam can guide people along the totally correct path
- although the message has been distorted, the originals were revelations from Allah and therefore should be respected
- however much the messages may have been changed and are no longer the originals, Muslims should respect Jews and Christians because they have 'part' of the truth. The Qur'an is quite clear that Jewish and Christian believers are to be recognised and given a special place because they are referred to as the 'People of the Book'.

Activities

2 Write a paragraph explaining Islamic teaching on holy books other than the Qur'an.

3 Find out what the Six Articles of Faith are for Muslims – what does this say about holy books other than the Qur'an?

ResultsPlus
Top Tip!

You can often improve your answer if you know the names of the three holy books mentioned and what Muslims believe they contain.

For discussion

Does it matter if the actual words may have changed? Is the meaning more important than the words?

Summary

Muslims believe that God revealed His message to prophets before Muhammad and that this was written down in holy books such as the tawrat, the zabur and the injil. However, over time, these books have been changed so much that they cannot be used as a guide for living. Only the Qur'an contains the full truth and final revelation from Allah.

1.10 The meaning and importance of belief in Islamic teaching on the revelation of the Qur'an to Muhammad

Learning outcomes

By the end of this lesson, you should be able to:

- outline what Muslims believe above the revelation of the Qur'an to Muhammad
- give your own opinion, with a reason, about this belief
- explain why this belief is important for Muslims
- evaluate different points of view about this belief, with reasons.

Many religious people believe that God can reveal himself in some way to humans either in visions, dreams or directly speaking to them. God is too powerful and holy for a human being to see.

The Night of Power

The most important event in the life of the Prophet was when he received the words of Allah for the first time.

Muhammad used to spend time alone in prayer and meditation. He was meditating one day as he usually did in a cave on Mount Hira. While he was there, and quite unexpectedly, he suddenly saw the Angel Jibril who commanded him to recite the words he could see before him. He had never been taught to read but he found that he could recite the words. These were the first five verses of Surah 96 in the Qur'an. The words remained engraved in his heart.

Activities

1 If you went to the theatre and looked at the stage before the play started you would only see the curtains. You would not know what the set was going to look like. All would be revealed (made clear) as soon as the curtains opened. Can you think of three other examples of things being revealed?

Activities

2 Look up Surah 96 (the first revelation) in the Qur'an. What do the words say about Allah?

For discussion

Why was this event a 'revelation'? What do you think is the difference between a revelation and an inspired idea?

How could the Prophet be sure that this was the true message of Allah?

Why is the revelation of the Qur'an to Muhammad so important for Muslims?

The revelation of the Qur'an to Muhammad is extremely important for Muslims because:

- it was the time when the first words of the Qur'an were revealed to Muhammad
- he became the final prophet of Allah because he had received this message from Allah
- it proves that the words in the Qur'an are the exact speech of Allah
- it was the beginning of many such revelations which went on for 23 years and formed the whole Qur'an
- for Muslims, this is the great miracle of Islam.

This event restored the original message, sent to many prophets over the centuries. There could be no mistaking this message because it came to the prophet directly from Allah. It was a miracle because Muhammad could recite the message even though he had not been taught to read. This message inspired the Prophet to teach it to others, to proclaim that there is no god but Allah, to show how worship should be offered to no other person or thing in the universe. Muhammad was chosen by Allah to be His messenger. This is what the words of the Shahadah (see page 60) proclaim.

Activities

Research the Prophet's life.

3 Find out what he did straight after this experience.
4 Who were the first people to accept his message?
5 Lots of people today claim to have messages from God. How can Muslims today be sure that the message of the Qur'an is from Allah?

ResultsPlus
Build Better Answers

Explain why the revelation of the Qur'an to Muhammad is important to Muslims. (8 marks)

 Basic, 1–2-mark answers

Basic answers usually describe what the Qur'an is or how it was revealed to Muhammad rather than giving reasons why the revelation is important to Muslims.

 Good, 3–6-mark answers

Level two answers (3–4 marks) tend to give two reasons without any development. Level three answers (5–6 marks) will explain the reasons.

▲ **Excellent, 7–8-mark answers**

Most excellent answers will give four reasons why the revelation of the Qur'an to Muhammad is important to Muslims. Other excellent answers will give fewer reasons but explain them. It is possible to get full marks by giving just one reason, but this would need to be explained in real depth.

Summary

The revelation of the Qur'an to Muhammad took 23 years. It began when the Angel Jibril visited Muhammad and told him to recite the words he could see, even though he had not been taught to read. This is known as the greatest miracle in Islam and is extremely important to Muslims.

1.11 How belief in akhirah affects the lives of Muslims

Learning outcomes

By the end of this lesson, you should be able to:

- know what the belief in akhirah is
- give your own opinion, with reasons, about belief in akhirah
- explain why the belief in akhirah is important for Muslims
- evaluate different points of view about this belief, with reasons.

What is akhirah?

Akhirah is the belief in life after death. It is one of the main beliefs of Islam. Muslims believe that our life on Earth is simply a preparation for a better life after death. The good will go to Paradise, described in the Qur'an as a garden with water and flowers, and the bad will go to Jahannam (Hell), a place of torment and pain. Death is like a gateway into the next world.

Activities

1 Why do you think Paradise is described in the Qur'an as a garden? What would be your idea of paradise? Imagine you have received an e-mail from a friend asking this question. Write your reply.

The opening words of the Qur'an are '*Praise be to Allah, The Cherisher and Sustainer of the Worlds, Most Gracious, Most Merciful, Master of the Day of Judgement*' (Surah 1:2–4).

Before entering this next life Muslims believe they will appear before Allah to be judged on the way they have lived their lives. Their book of deeds in which all their actions during life are recorded (see pages 16–17) will be opened and presented to them.

Allah is in control of the world and has given human beings the responsibility to look after it. Allah will judge how each individual has fulfilled their duty on a day at the end of time, the Day of Judgement. No one knows when this will be.

Life on Earth
Life is a test from Allah. Nothing can happen without Allah's knowledge. How we deal with the test will determine what happens after death

Death
Death is returning to Allah and not something to be feared

Barzakh
Barzakh is a place where souls wait until the Day of Judgement. The word means 'barrier' and divides the living from the dead

Judgement
On the Day of Judgement everyone will stand alone before Allah. It will be too late for forgiveness. No one else can help you now, what you have done is your responsibility alone.
'(It will be) the Day when no soul shall have power (to do) aught for another…' (Surah 82:19)

Paradise   **Jahannam**

Paradise is described as a garden.

Those who die before the Day of Judgement are taken to a place of waiting, Barzakh.

How does this belief affect the life of a Muslim?

Imagine that instead of your forehead you had a computer screen that showed all your thoughts and recorded all your actions so that everyone could see exactly what you were like as a person. Nothing would be hidden. In a way, that is how Muslims have to live their lives as they believe Allah is aware of everything. Nothing can be hidden from Allah. During life it is possible to ask forgiveness for any wrong thoughts or actions, but after death that is no longer possible.

Activities

2 With a partner discuss how this might affect how you live your life. Go back over the last week. Without going into detail, are there things you wish you had not done or things you wished you had done? Would it have made a difference if you knew someone was going to check on you? Give reasons for your answers.

The belief that Allah is 'closer than your jugular vein' gives Muslims a great sense of 'God-consciousness' (taqwa). It alters a Muslim's motivation for doing things. For Muslims, everything they do is an act of ibadah, worship of Allah, so it should be done to the best of their ability – both small things like helping at home and large things like caring for the poor. Life on Earth is a test. Everybody has good and bad things happen to them, but it is how you react in these situations that will determine if you pass the test and are rewarded in Paradise.

So Muslims will aim to:

- observe the Five Pillars (see page 61)
- learn the Qur'an (see pages 38–39)
- follow Shari'ah (see pages 90–91) and avoid things that are haram
- show kindness to others
- work hard in a job that is acceptable to Allah
- be honest and fair in every aspect of life
- do every action for the pleasure of Allah.

Activities

3 Imagine that you have found a diary written by a Muslim teenager. Note down any actions recorded in it that could be seen as helping them to pass the test of life.

For Muslims this belief in akhirah is a positive thing. It gives a meaning and purpose to their lives. It is good to know that there is a supreme God who cares for His people. It is also good to know that Allah is merciful and will forgive them if things go wrong. Remember, the only unforgiveable sin is shirk (see pages 6–7).

For discussion

'We should do good because we want to, not for a reward.' Discuss this and give reasons for your point of view.

Summary

The belief in akhirah gives Muslims a meaning and purpose in life because they are preparing for the Day of Judgement when they will be rewarded or punished for the way they have lived on Earth.

Quick quiz

1 Name three prophets in Islam apart from Muhammad.

2 What is meant by 'Islam'?

3 What event is called the 'Night of Power'?

4 What does 'akhirah' mean?

5 What is the 'tawrat'?

6 What is the major sin in Islam?

7 What is meant by 'tawhid'?

8 Give two things Muslims believe about angels.

9 Give two reasons why the compassion and mercy of Allah are important to Muslims.

10 What is meant by 'al-Qadar'?

Find out more

This book is preparing you to take a GCSE examination. To get the best marks you need to be able to develop different points of view. If possible, contact a Muslim group in your area and explain that you would like to talk to them about their beliefs to help you with your examination. This will help you give a clear Muslim viewpoint. If you are a Muslim, then it would be useful to talk to a member of another religion or a non-religious person so that you can give an alternative point of view to your own on these matters.

Student tips

As a non-Muslim I found lots of the vocabulary really difficult in this topic. I found that it really helped me to make cards with the key terms on one side and the definitions on the back and to use them to test myself or get friends to test me. It really paid off in the exam as I found I could use the key terms in answering the (c) questions as well as defining them in the (a) questions – I'm sure my key term cards helped me to get such good marks!

Plenary activity

All the parts of Section 1 depend on you understanding the importance of the belief in tawhid. It is the basis of everything else in Muslim belief. Go back through the section and identify one idea in each topic that links with the belief in tawhid.

Self-evaluation checklist

How well have you understood the topics in this section? In the first column of the table below use the following code to rate your understanding:

Green – I understand this fully.

Orange – I am confident I can answer most questions on this.

Red – I need to do a lot more work on this topic.

In the second and third columns you need to think about:

- whether you have an opinion on this topic and could give reasons for that opinion, if asked.
- whether you can give the opinion of someone who disagrees with you and give reasons for this alternative opinion.

Content covered	My understanding is red/orange/ green	Can I give my opinion?	Can I give an alternative opinion?
The nature of belief in tawhid			
Why belief in tawhid is important for Muslims			
What is meant by shirk			
Why shirk is a major sin in Islam			
What is meant by the creativity of Allah			
Why belief in the creativity of Allah is important for Muslims			
The Islamic teaching on the nature of humans as khalifah			
Why this is important to Muslims			
The meaning of Islamic teaching on al-Qadar and human freedom			
Why al-Qadar and human freedom are important for Muslims			
The meaning of Islamic teaching on angels			
Why angels are important for Muslims			
The meaning of risalah			
Why risalah is important for Muslims			
The meaning of Islamic teaching on holy books other than the Qur'an (the tawrat, the zabur, the injil)			
The importance of holy books other than the Qur'an for Muslims			
The meaning of the revelation of the Qur'an to Muhammad			
Why the revelation of the Qur'an to Muhammad is important for Muslims			
How belief in akhirah affects the lives of Muslims			

examzone

KnowZone
Beliefs and values

Introduction

In the exam you will see a choice of two questions on this module. Each question will include four tasks, which test your knowledge, understanding and evaluation of the material covered. A 2-mark question will ask you to define a term; a 4-mark question will ask your opinion on a point of view; an 8-mark question will ask you to explain a particular belief or idea; a 6-mark question will ask for your opinion on a point of view and ask you to consider an alternative point of view.

You must give your opinion, but must also include the reasons for your opinion. You need to give two reasons – any more than this and you will be wasting valuable time.

This question is always split into two parts and you should answer each part separately. For at least one of the parts you must refer to Muslim beliefs, and it's probably a good idea to consider what Muslims think first and then either use that for your own opinion or for the alternative opinion in (ii).

Mini exam paper

(a) What is **tawhid**? (2 marks)

(b) Do you think Allah created the universe?

Give **two** reasons for your point of view. (4 marks)

(c) Explain why risalah is important for Muslims. (8 marks)

(d) 'Muslims are free to do what they like with their lives.'

In your answer you should refer to Islam.

   (i) Do you agree? Give reasons for your opinion. (3 marks)

   (ii) Give reasons why some people may disagree with you. (3 marks)

Give a glossary definition. You do not need to write any more – often this can be done in one sentence.

This question is worth the most so it is important that you spend some time on it. 'Explain why' means that you need to give reasons. A good answer here will often give four reasons, but you could give fewer reasons and still produce a good response if you develop them. This is also the question where you should double-check the quality of your spelling and punctuation. Remember to take care when writing your answers, and to use proper sentences and not bullet points.

Mark scheme

(a) You will earn **2 marks** for a correct answer, and **1 mark** for a partially correct answer.

(b) To earn up to the full **4 marks** you need to give two reasons (as asked) and develop them. Two brief reasons or one developed reason will earn **2 marks** and one reason without development will earn **1 mark**.

(c) You can earn **7–8 marks** by giving up to four reasons, but the fewer reasons you give, the more you must develop them. You are being assessed on your use of language, so you also need to take care to express your understanding in a clear style of English and make some use of specialist vocabulary.

(d) To go beyond **3 marks** for the whole of this question you must refer to Islam. The more you are able to develop your reasons the more marks you will earn. Three simple reasons can earn you the same mark as one developed reason.

ResultsPlus
Build Better Answers

(c) Explain why risalah is important for Muslims. (8 marks)

Student answer	Comments	Improved student answer
There are lots of prophets in Islam and they are important as they brought messages from Allah. They showed that the message was the same all the time.	This answer would get four marks for two basic reasons. A (c)-type exam question needs four reasons or two reasons that have been developed.	There are a lot of prophets in Islam and they are important as they brought messages from Allah. They all brought the same message which showed that it had not changed. Their message was that Allah was the only God and showed that Islam was the true religion. They also prepared the way for the final prophet Muhammad with the final message.

Community and tradition

Introduction

In this section you will study the way the idea of the community of believers – the ummah – is linked to many aspects of Islam. To Muslims, Islam is more than just a faith, it is a way of life based on the teachings of the Qur'an and the example of the Prophet. It would not be possible to say you were a Muslim and yet not accept the teachings of the Qur'an.

Following this way of life and belonging to the ummah is also a source of identity for Muslims.

The teachings of the Qur'an are explained by the way Muhammad lived. He has been described as 'the Qur'an in practice'. He is the perfect example to follow because the Qur'an was revealed directly to him.

Learning outcomes for this section
By the end of this section you should be able to:

- give definitions of the key terms and use them in answer to GCSE questions
- understand the meaning and importance of belief in Muhammad as the Seal of the Prophets
- understand why the Qur'an has supreme authority for Muslims
- understand how and why Muslims show respect for the Qur'an
- understand and evaluate the importance of the Shari'ah for Muslims
- evaluate the importance and effects of the ummah
- explain the reasons for the main features of a mosque
- understand and evaluate the role of the imam in a mosque
- evaluate the role and importance of the mosque for the local Muslim community
- understand and explain the reasons for the differences between Sunni and Shi'ah communities
- evaluate the role and importance of Muslim groups and movements in British mosques
- understand different attitudes to Sufi forms of worship.

edexcel ▦ key terms

authority	masjid	sunnah
bismillah	qadi	Sunni
hadith	Shari'ah	ulama
imam	Shi'ah	ummah

Fascinating fact

The first mosque in the UK was built in Wales in 1860. Now, 150 years later, there are over 1,000 mosques, with one in nearly every city in the UK.

31

مسجد عمر

For discussion

Many buildings and groups can be identified by how they look. How far is this important? What other things might help you identify a particular group?

1 Make a list of the different groups you belong to and next to each one write what it is that identifies the group. For example, next to 'school' you might write 'uniform'.

2 Look at the picture on this page. What is it? How do you know?

2.1 The meaning and importance of belief in Muhammad as the Seal of the Prophets

Learning outcomes

By the end of this lesson, you should be able to:

- state what Muslims believe about Muhammad as the Seal of the Prophets
- give your own opinion, with a reason, about the importance of this belief to Muslims
- explain why this belief is important for Muslims
- evaluate, with reasons, different points of view about this belief.

edexcel ⠿ key terms

hadith – Sayings and actions of the Prophet Muhammad as recorded by his family and friends.

sunnah – The sayings and deeds of the Prophet.

In 610 CE Muhammad was praying alone when he heard a voice calling his name. He also heard the command 'to recite'. He saw a scroll but was unable to read it as he had not been taught to read (see pages 22–23). This is important because Muhammad could not have collected the words of the Qur'an from any other book. Muslims believe that he was receiving the first of a series of direct messages from Allah, which continued for the next 23 years. This event is recorded in Surah 96 in the Qur'an.

Activities

1 The prophet Muhammad was born in Makkah. Find out as much as you can about his early life before he received the first revelation from Allah.

What is meant by the 'Seal of the Prophets'?

One of the meanings of the word 'seal' is 'to close finally and irrevocably' (once and for all time). This means that it is finished and nothing will be added to it. Also, a seal is used on a document to show the authority (see pages 34–35) of the person sending it.

Activities

2 Make a list of anything you can think of that is (a) sealed to prove it is finished and (b) given a seal to show it has the writer's authority.

A seal means that the message has not been tampered with.

Muslims believe that throughout history Allah has sent messengers and messages to people around the world in order to teach them how to live at a particular time. There are 25 prophets mentioned by name in the Qur'an. These men are accepted within Islam as having contributed to God revealing himself to mankind. However, Muslims believe that, as time progressed, their messages became distorted and so a new messenger was sent.

Muhammad is also called a prophet, but his role was different. The message he received from Allah was the culmination of all the other messages and was given to him directly by Allah in Arabic. Muhammad would recite the words he received from Allah and his companions would write them down. Muslims believe that the Arabic words of the Qur'an they read today have remained unchanged from the time of Muhammad.

Why is Muhammad so important?

Muhammad lived his life totally as Allah commanded in the Qur'an so he is the most important person for Muslims as a role model. He sets the example of:

- how to live the Muslim life
- how to be a faithful servant of Allah
- how to keep on the straight path of Islam.

That is why Muslims try to follow his example (**sunnah**) and why they often refer to his sayings and actions. These were collected together by his companions and written down in collections called **hadith**.

For discussion

Why do you think Muhammad is referred to as 'the Seal of the Prophets' (Surah 33:40)? Why was he different from all the other prophets? What do you think this means for Muslims today?

Why is this belief important for Muslims?

For Muslims, all the prophets of Allah are important. This is because they brought to people the true message of Allah for their time and for their own communities. Muhammad is also one of the prophets, but with these differences:

- he completed the message of Allah
- he is the last prophet Allah will send
- he brought the message of Allah for all people and for all times.

This is why he is called 'the Seal of the Prophets'.

Activities

Muslims learn about the life of the Prophet from an early age. You may remember incidents from the life of the Prophet that you looked up earlier.

3   Some events in the life of the Prophet are particularly important today. Why are these events important. Copy and complete the table below.

Event	Reason it is important to Muslims today
The Night of Power	
The migration to Madinah	
His leadership of the community in Madinah	
His last pilgrimage	
His last speech to his followers before his death	

Although Muhammad is regarded as the best example of how to follow the teachings of Allah, Muslims will never give him equal status with Allah because that would be the sin of shirk. Muslims are also very careful to avoid pictures of the Prophet.

For discussion

Why do you think Muslims never have pictures of the Prophet?

Which of these words do you think a Muslim would use and which would they avoid when they speak about their relationship with the Prophet?

- respect
- honour
- fear
- veneration
- love
- worship
- devotion

Summary

In the Qur'an Muhammad is described as the Seal of the Prophets because he was given the final message from Allah to mankind. Allah said that Muhammad would be the last prophet.

2.2 Why the Qur'an has supreme authority for Muslims

Learning outcomes

By the end of this lesson you should be able to:

- state what Muslims believe about the authority of the Qur'an
- give your own opinion, with reasons, about this belief
- explain why this belief is important for Muslims
- evaluate different points of view, with reasons, about why the Qur'an has supreme authority for Muslims.

edexcel **::: key terms**

authority – The power and right to make demands of others.

bismillah – The words that begin every surah.

Schools, families, countries and even groups of friends have rules (written and unwritten) that help them live together. Some of these rules are more important than others: breaking some of them may lead to punishment.

Activities

Think about what rules you obey in life and who makes the rules.

1 Draw an ideas map, with you in the middle and the rules round the outside. Add to your map who made the rule, for example parents, school, law of the country.

2 With a partner discuss why you keep some of these rules.

3 Make a list of the reasons and then decide which reason is the most important.

For discussion

Some people in our lives have more **authority** than others. What gives them this authority? Give reasons for your answer.

For Muslims it is the Qur'an that is the most important source of guidance for their lives. The Qur'an is made up of 114 surahs (chapters), containing about 6,000 verses. It is divided into 30 sections called juz as well as seven sections called manzil, so a Muslim could recite the whole Qur'an in one month or one week if they wished.

Muslims read the Qur'an in Arabic.

Every chapter of the Qur'an except one begins with these words, known as the **bismillah**:

In the name of Allah
Most Gracious
Most Merciful

Activities

4 Find out which surah does not begin with the bismillah and why.

Why does the Qur'an have supreme authority for Muslims?

- Muslims believe that it contains the exact words of Allah:
  This is very important because Muslims believe that the other holy books mentioned in the Qur'an have lost the original wording and have been changed over the years so are no longer accurate.

- It was brought to people through the final prophet:
  Although Allah had sent prophets with his message before to different people at different times (see pages 20–21), this time the message was for all people for all time and would not be repeated.

- It was recited exactly, word for word, by the Prophet:
  Muslims believe that as the Prophet received the revelations, he recited them exactly and then the words were recorded immediately and accurately by his companions.

- It has never been changed:
  Muslims read the Qur'an in the original Arabic so that they are sure their knowledge is correct. Many Muslim scholars think that the Qur'an should never be translated into other languages because of the risk of mistakes.

- It is the first great miracle for Muslims:
  Muslims believe that Muhammad had not been taught to read and write and so could not have written the Qur'an, so it is a miracle from Allah.

Nobody is forced to follow the teaching of the Qur'an. Muslims show their faith in Allah by accepting its **authority**. They receive it as guidance about how to live as faithful Muslims. Also, those who follow its teachings experience for themselves that it is true. They discover that it works.

Here are some of the other reasons why Muslims accept its authority:

- It helps them to understand the qualities of Allah, shown in the 99 names.
- It shows them how to follow the straight path.
- It inspires them to struggle in the cause of Allah.

- It gives them a framework of belief about Allah and about their own lives.
- It encourages them through the example of faithful believers.
- It offers them support and help in times of need and hardship.
- It gives warnings to those who do not believe.

For discussion

Review the information you read in Section 1 pages 20–21 on the teachings of Islam concerning other holy books.

Why do Muslims believe that the Qur'an is different?

ResultsPlus
Build Better Answers

Explain why the Qur'an has supreme authority for Muslims. (8 marks)

▪ **Basic, 1–2-mark answers**

Basic answers usually describe how the Qur'an is treated rather than giving reasons why it has supreme authority for Muslims.

● **Good, 3–6-mark answers**

Level two answers (3–4 marks) tend to give two reasons without any development. Level three answers (5–6 marks) will explain the reasons given or give more of them.

▲ **Excellent, 7–8-mark answers**

Most excellent answers will give four reasons. Other excellent answers will give fewer reasons but develop them. It is possible to get full marks by giving just one reason, but this would need to be explained in real depth.

Summary

The Qur'an is the supreme authority for Muslims because they believe it is the word of Allah.

2.3 How and why Muslims show respect for the Qur'an

36

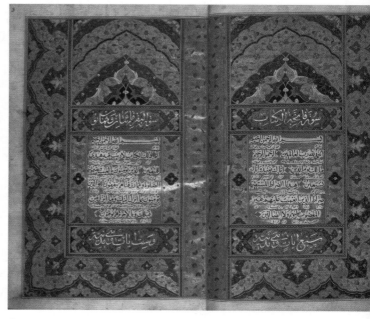

Beautiful decoration to show that the Qur'an is special.

Learning outcomes

By the end of this lesson, you should be able to:

● outline how Muslims show respect for the Qur'an

● give your own opinion, with reasons, about this practice

● explain why showing respect for the Qur'an is important for Muslims

● evaluate, with reasons, different points of view about this belief.

The Qur'an is the complete book of guidance for Muslims, and they believe that each word was revealed to Muhammad and has remained unchanged over the centuries. It is literally the word of God. This means that it must be treated with respect.

Activities

1 The word 'respect' means to show special attention to something, to care for something.

Who or what do you respect? Complete the spider diagram.

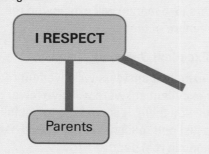

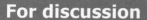

For discussion

How do these pictures show that the Qur'an is being treated with respect?

Why do Muslims show respect for the Qur'an?

The Qur'an might appear to some as just like any other book. Muslims would never dream of treating it like any other book, though, because its message is so special to them. This is because they believe it contains the actual words and the message of Allah. It is this that makes it sacred, rather than the paper on which it is written, or the cover on the outside. The message of the Qur'an is written in beautiful handwriting, called calligraphy, and people have been specially trained to write in this way.

Calligraphy.   *Qur'an in a special cover.*

How do Muslims show that the Qur'an is a special book?

1 Before reading or touching the Qur'an a Muslim must:

- perform wudu (ritual washing)
- make sure they are in the right frame of mind to read it.

2 When the Qur'an is being recited, Muslims must:

- not speak
- not eat or drink.

3 When not being read the Qur'an must be:

- covered to protect it from dust
- put in a high place so that nothing is placed on top of it.

For discussion

Do you think non-Muslims should also show respect for the Qur'an? Give reasons for your point of view.

Are these actions enough?

It is possible to show respect in all the ways described above and still not really respect the Qur'an. It is what one is thinking that is also important.

Many Muslims think the most important way of showing respect for the Qur'an is by making sure that they are:

- listening to and understanding its teaching
- remembering the teaching of Allah
- and, most importantly, applying this teaching in their lives.

Qur'ans on the highest shelf .

Build Better Answers

'Nobody should base their lives on a book written hundreds of years ago.'
In your answer you should refer to Islam.
(i) Do you agree? Give reasons for your opinion. (3 marks)
(ii) Explain why some people might disagree with you. (3 marks)

These comments apply to both parts.

▪ **Basic, 1-mark answers**

These answers will give one basic reason. Be aware of the difference between saying what you think and giving reasons why you think it.

● **Good, 2-mark answers**

These will either give two brief reasons or one developed reason. 'Developed' means you say something extra to explain your reason.

▲ **Excellent, 3-mark answers**

Answers that get full marks will either give three brief reasons or two developed reasons. They could also give one reason, but this would need to be fully-developed.

Activities

2 Why do you think it is important for Muslims to have the right intention when they prepare to read the Qur'an?

3 Return to the words in 'for discussion' on pages 32–33 about attitudes to Muhammad. Which words also apply to the attitudes Muslims have towards the Qur'an?

Summary

Muslims believe the Qur'an contains the words of Allah and is not just a book like any other book, so they treat it with great respect.

2.4 The nature and importance of the Shari'ah for Muslims

Learning outcomes

By the end of this lesson, you should be able to:

- outline what the Shari'ah is
- give your own opinion, with reasons, about the nature and importance of the Shari'ah
- explain why the Shari'ah is important for Muslims
- evaluate different points of view about the nature and importance of the Shari'ah, with reasons.

edexcel ::: key terms

qadi – A judge in Islamic law.

Shari'ah – Islamic law based on the Qur'an and sunnah.

ulama – Scholars of Islamic law and jurisprudence (the study of law).

Activities

1   Newspapers print stories about punishments that are given under Shari'ah law. These often give a very negative view of it. Find out more about Shari'ah and its influence in the UK by going to www.pearsonschoolsandfecolleges.co.uk/hotlinks (express code 4264P) and clicking on the 'Find out more about Shari'ah' link.

'*Verily, this is My Way, leading straight: follow it: do not follow (other) paths: they will scatter you about from His (great) Path…*' (Surah 6:153)

For discussion

Look at the pictures above. Imagine each way will get you to your destination. Which would be the easiest to follow and find your way? How would you decide?

If you had been told that there were hidden mines along the road, what would you do?

The Qur'an describes Islam as a straight path, with the idea that, if you follow this path carefully, you will please Allah. Keeping to the path will help you avoid dangers that may harm you. It is the quickest and most straightforward way to your goal, which is to please Allah. On this path, you will be following the same guidance as other Muslims, and this will give you courage and make you feel you are on the right path.

The **Shari'ah** is the word used to describe this straight path. It consists of a large collection of rules about how Muslims should behave in every part of their lives. Among these rules are clear instructions about which actions in life are permitted and which are forbidden. It covers everything from prayer and fasting to helping the poor. You will learn about these in Section 4.

The Shari'ah is not simply a large code of rules. It is also an ongoing path, or a process, that is still happening today, but that began with the Qur'an.

The Qur'an is the first and most important book of guidance for Muslims. It contains the first principles on which all Shari'ah law is based.

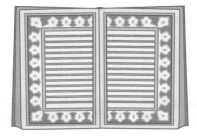

But as the Muslim community grew and expanded, new guidance was needed for new situations.

For this guidance, the early Muslim community looked to the traditions (sunnah) about the Prophet and especially his recorded sayings and teachings (hadith). The community used these to help to interpret and apply the principles in the Qur'an.

Gradually, this guidance was gathered together in books of laws, which form the basis of the Shari'ah. From these came a number of schools of law, with their own judges (qadi) who helped to administer the law. Islamic law is a huge area of study in itself.

Shari'ah today

Today, in a quickly changing world where new issues and problems arise, it is important for Muslims to know how the Shari'ah should be applied. A group of scholars (**ulama**) who are experts in Islamic law will see if they can find anything in the Shari'ah that is similar to the new issue they have to consider. They use this example or analogy (qiyyas) to help them decide what the rules should be. They also consult each other and earlier laws to try to arrive at an agreed interpretation or consensus (ijma). When this has been done, they issue a ruling (fatwa). Thus the law continues to develop.

Why is Shari'ah important for Muslims

Muhammad is reported to have said that Allah does not accept belief unless it is expressed in deeds and that a person's deeds will only be acceptable to Him if they represent beliefs. Muslims follow the teaching of Shari'ah because they believe that:

- Allah is always aware of what they are doing and thinking
- everyone will be judged at the end of life on their beliefs and deeds.

Shari'ah in non-Muslim countries

Many Muslims, including those who live in the UK, find themselves in a country where the 'law of the land' has developed in a very different way from the Shari'ah. Sometimes there are differences in the law, and often the law does not deal with matters that are of concern to Muslims. However, most Muslims living in a non-Muslim country ensure they follow the Shari'ah and the law of the land at the same time without any problems.

Summary

Shari'ah is Islamic law that helps Muslims to follow the path Allah has set for them.

2.5 The importance and effects of the ummah

Learning outcomes

By the end of this lesson, you should be able to:

- outline how the ummah influences the lives of Muslims
- give your own opinion, with reasons, about the importance and effects of the ummah
- explain why the ummah is important for Muslims
- evaluate different points of view about the ummah, with reasons.

edexcel ::: key terms

ummah – The worldwide Muslim community.

'Hold fast all together by the rope which Allah stretches out for you and be not divided among yourselves' (Surah 3:103)

For discussion

Do you think it is important for everyone to belong to a community? Give reasons for your answer.

Activities

1 How many different kinds of people are shown in the various groups in the pictures below? What do these pictures show about the way Muslims regard each other? What is it that they all have in common?

At the beginning of this section you thought about the different groups you belong to and what gives them a special identity. All over the world people belong to different religious groups. Most of these religions are made up of people from different backgrounds, races and cultures. Each group has its own beliefs and practices that make it a community.

Islam, as a worldwide religion, is also a community of believers who come from different backgrounds, races and cultures who all believe in Islam.

The ummah praying together.

The ummah sharing.

The ummah celebrating.

Muslims in the UK belong to a lot of different communities. They belong to the community of people who live in their own part of town or area of a city. They mix with them when they shop, at work and during leisure activities. They also belong to the community of Muslims who live in the area. Often these communities have been there for quite a long time. In fact, sometimes there are many different Muslim communities who live in an area. They tend to meet and mix with those they share a language with, or who have settled in the UK after migrating from the same part of the world. These groups of Muslims may go to different mosques where they will be with other Muslims they know and understand. Some Muslims who live in big cities will go to mosques where there are Muslims of many different backgrounds, languages and cultures all meeting together. Whatever groups or communities Muslims are part of, they all belong to the one worldwide community of Islam, the **ummah**.

Reasons why the ummah is important

The idea of one worldwide community is very important in Islam because:

- Islam unites all Muslims everywhere, no matter what their race or culture
- having one worldwide community reflects the Oneness of Allah (tawhid, see pages 4–5)
- the ummah helps and gives strength to individual Muslims
- many of the aspects of being a Muslim are communal in nature.

How do Muslims show the importance of the ummah?

The Prophet said that believers are like the parts of a building as each part supports the others.

- At prayer:
  All Muslims face the qiblah, the direction of the Ka'bah in Makkah, which is often referred to as the house of Allah. The Ka'bah is like the hub of Islam. Wherever you are in the world, if you visit a mosque you will see almost exactly the same

actions of the salah performed when Muslims pray. It is another feature that expresses the unity of the Muslim community.

- Reading the Qur'an:
  Muslims around the world speak many different languages, but when they read the Qur'an and when they pray they use the language of Arabic, whatever their native language is. This helps to strengthen the sense of unity in the ummah.

- Giving zakah (see pages 66–67):
  Every year Muslims give a percentage of their wealth to help other people because wealth is a gift from Allah and must be shared.

- Going on hajj (see pages 74–77):
  On the pilgrimage to Makkah over two million Muslims gather from every country in the world to worship Allah. It does not matter whether you are black or white, rich or poor, male or female, everyone is equal in the sight of Allah. Here the unity of the ummah is shown very clearly.

ResultsPlus
Build Better Answers

Do you think that the Five Pillars of Islam unite the ummah?
Give **two** reasons for your point of view. (4 marks)

■ **Basic, 1-mark answers**
These answers would give an opinion but supported by one simple reason.

● **Good, 2–3-mark answers**
Good answers will support their opinion with one developed and one simple reason.

▲ **Excellent, 4-mark answers**
Excellent answers will support their opinion with two developed reasons.

Summary

Muslims, regardless of their race, culture, sex, age or background are united as one community who belong to Allah. This is called the ummah.

2.6 The main features of a mosque and the reasons for them

Learning outcomes

By the end of this lesson you should be able to:

● outline the main features and purposes of a mosque

● give your own opinion, with reasons, about the design of mosques

● explain why the features of a mosque are important for Muslims

● evaluate different points of view about the design of mosques, with reasons.

Activities

1 Is there a place that is special to you? Close your eyes and imagine being there. Write two sentences about how you feel when you visit this place.

Many people like to spend time alone thinking about their lives and sometimes praying to God. Some people find that going to a special place, which might be quiet or beautiful, helps them to do this.

What is a mosque?

The Arabic word for 'mosque', a Muslim place of worship, is **masjid**. It means a place where people prostrate themselves, or bow down. That gives a clue about its purpose.

The whole idea of having a quiet place set aside for Muslims to pray began in the time of the Prophet himself. In fact, Muhammad was responsible for building the first mosque in the city of Madinah, after his journey to escape his persecutors in Makkah. A mosque still stands on this site today.

It is important to remember that wherever Muslims bow down to pray, that is a mosque. That means that the place set aside for prayer at home is a mosque. Ordinary houses can be used as mosques, and many Muslims in the UK continue to pray in houses that have been adapted as mosques.

edexcel ::: key terms

masjid – Place of prostration.

Muhammad taught that wherever a person is at the hour of prayer they should pray: that place becomes a mosque.

ResultsPlus
Build Better Answers

'Muslims do not need a mosque to pray to Allah.'
In your answer you should refer to Islam.
(i) Do you agree? Give reasons for your point of view. (3 marks)
(ii) Give reasons why some people might disagree with you. (3 marks)

These comments apply to both parts.

■ **Basic, 1-mark answers**

These answers will give one basic reason. Be aware of the difference between saying what you think and giving reasons why you think it.

● **Good, 2-mark answers**

These will either give two brief reasons or one developed reason. 'Developed' means you say something extra to explain your reason.

▲ **Excellent, 3-mark answers**

These will give three brief reasons or two developed reasons.

Features of a mosque

However, many Muslims in the UK and around the world pray in specially built mosques.

Dome: many Muslims think of this as a symbol of space and therefore of the universe that Allah has created.

Minaret: a tall tower from which worshippers are called to prayer. Part of that call to prayer reminds Muslims that they are being summoned into the presence of Allah, with the words 'Allahu akbar' – God is most great.

Men and women are separated during prayer. Sometimes the women will stand behind the men but often there are separate prayer areas for them.

Mihrab: one wall of the prayer hall in a mosque has a niche or alcove (mihrab), which shows the direction (qiblah) of the Ka'bah, the house of God in Makkah. All Muslims should face in this direction when they pray to Allah.

Minbar: a small platform from which the leader of the prayers gives a talk to remind worshippers of their duty to Allah.

Many mosques are beautifully decorated with patterns and designs such as the great mosque in Makkah with the Ka'bah in the courtyard, but you will not see pictures of people, and certainly not any pictures of the Prophet. Many of the designs are verses from the Qur'an written in calligraphy.

There will also be a place for washing inside the mosque. When Muslims come to pray, both the place where they pray and they themselves must be clean and pure, outwardly and inwardly, because Allah is holy. Men and women have separate washrooms.

The purpose behind the design of a mosque is to provide a space where:

- there is an atmosphere of peace and tranquillity
- worshippers can concentrate on Allah, without any distractions
- the dirt and bustle of daily life are left outside and Muslims can feel a sense of purity as they stand before Allah.

Summary

A mosque is a building where Muslims can go to pray. Many mosques have special features in them to help Muslims concentrate their thoughts on Allah.

2.7 The role and importance of the imam in a mosque

44

Learning outcomes

By the end of this lesson you should be able to:

- outline the main roles of an imam in a mosque
- give your own opinion with reasons on these roles
- explain why the imam is important in a mosque
- evaluate different points of view about the importance of imams, with reasons.

key terms

imam – A person who leads salah prayers (five compulsory daily prayers).

ResultsPlus
Watch out!

Never call an imam a 'priest' – this will not give the impression that you fully understand what an imam does!

For discussion

What is the role of an imam?

Activities

1 Look at the picture and describe what you think the role is of the person standing in front of the group.

The **imam** is chosen by the congregation. The only qualification is that he is a devout and committed Muslim who is well trained in the teaching of the Qur'an and is often able to recite the whole Qur'an from memory. In many larger mosques throughout the world, leading the prayers is the only thing an imam is appointed to do.

1 The word 'imam' refers simply to the person who stands in front of others and leads them in the formal prayers (salah). The people follow his movements and listen to his words, which tell them when to move to the next stage of their prayers. This is especially important for the Jum'ah prayers on Fridays, the main prayers around midday when all Muslim men in the community are expected to pray together in a congregation.

2 At the Friday congregational prayers the imam usually gives a sermon (khutbah) in two parts, one before the prayers and addressed to everyone in the most common language spoken by those who attend. The other part of the sermon comes at the beginning of the actual prayers and is recited formally by the imam in Arabic.

The sermon is important because the imam will outline some teaching from the Qur'an and then explain its meaning and how it should be applied by Muslims today in their daily lives.

3 The imam will help children from an early age to learn to recite portions of the Qur'an, to understand its teaching, to learn some Arabic so that they can later take part in the prayers, and to learn about the basic teachings of Islam.

4 The imam gives advice and counselling on many issues that Muslims face in the UK today.

5 The imam leads prayers at weddings and funerals.

6 The imam visits those who are sick or in prison.

An imam teaching Qur'anic studies.

It is not usually the imam's role to 'run the mosque' in terms of daily organisation – that is normally done by a mosque committee, often the same group of people who appoint the imam in the first place.

The importance of the imam

The main reasons why the imam is an important figure in Islam are:

- prayer is important and leading the prayer is the key role of the imam
- the imam ensures that children learn about Islam

- the imam helps Muslims to apply the rules of Shari'ah law in their daily lives and so makes sure that they follow what is halal and reject what is haram (see pages 90–91)
- the imam extends the ummah by giving guidance and instruction to new converts to Islam
- as an important role model for the Muslim community, the imam shows how to live as a faithful Muslim in a non-Muslim society
- the imam makes sure that the message of Islam is kept pure and is not influenced by the values of secular western culture
- the imam often represents the Muslim community in its dealings with other local political and religious groups.

There has been much debate recently about the training of imams for working in British mosques. Some Muslims argue that the training should be given in traditional Qur'anic colleges in mainly Muslim countries where the training will not be influenced by 'Western' ideas and values. Others argue that imams cannot communicate properly with young Muslims who have been born and have grown up in the UK, unless they are fluent in English and have gone through the UK education system.

Activities

2 Sort the reasons why the role of an imam is important into the most and least important reasons. Explain your ranking to a partner.

For discussion

'All imams working in the UK should be trained in the UK.'

Do you agree? Give reasons for your opinion.

Summary

An imam is a person who provides guidance to other Muslims to follow the Five Pillars and live in accordance with the teaching of Allah.

2.8 The role and importance of the mosque for the local Muslim community

46

Learning outcomes

By the end of this lesson you should be able to:

- outline the role of the mosque in the local community
- give your own opinion, with reasons, about this role
- explain why the mosque is important for the local Muslim community
- evaluate different points of view about the importance of the mosque, with reasons.

Activities

1 Do you remember what it is like to start at a new school and how long it took to feel you belonged to that school? With a partner make a list of the things that helped to make you feel that you were a member of the school community.

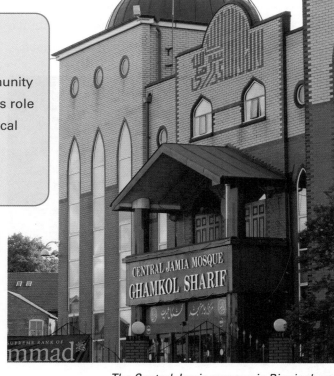

The Central Jamia mosque in Birmingham.

As large numbers of Muslims from around the world started to settle in parts of the UK, they felt the need for a place that would be familiar and where they could gain a sense of community, as well as a place that would identify them clearly with their religion, Islam.

Most of the early meeting places for Muslims in the UK were mosques based in family homes.

Recently, a number of fine, modern mosques have been built, keeping some of the traditional style of mosques around the world but also adapting them to the conditions of living in the UK. Some of these mosques cater for the needs of Muslims who belong to certain movements or groups within Islam. Others have been created to draw Muslims together from all areas of a city, and to include visitors from other cities and countries, with different languages, who wish to worship there – as well as people from different groups within the Muslim community. These mosques are cosmopolitan.

Birmingham Central Mosque.

Activities

2 Find out about a purpose-built mosque in your nearest city. Make a list of the activities that take place there and for each one write down how you think this helps the local Muslim community.

What happens at a mosque?

Most non-Muslims tend to think of the mosque as a building where Muslims go to worship Allah. Certainly this is true because every mosque will have a prayer room that will be prepared and set aside for prayer at certain times of the day.

However, a mosque is much more than this. Most mosques also act as a community centre where Muslims can gather for a large number of activities including weddings and funerals. The mosque provides a meeting place for all sorts of people in the local community, such as elderly Muslims, young Muslim families, student and youth groups and support groups for unemployed people. Many mosques have a strong network of support for the local community.

Most mosques run a madrasah and some large mosques have their own libraries for students to study in, a morgue (where bodies are prepared for burial), and nurseries. In some there is an office for the local Citizens Advice Bureau to help with problems and usually an imam is available to discuss issues of daily concern.

Activities

3 Design a poster advertising the work and facilities of a mosque.

Why mosques are important for the Muslim community

Nearly all Muslims in the UK think that their local mosque is an important feature in their lives. Here are some of the reasons they may give to explain this:

- A sense of identity – local Muslims have a strong sense of belonging to the worldwide ummah, but they need to express that sense of belonging in the community of Muslims where they live. It helps them to feel confident in being Muslims in a non-Muslim country.
- A feeling of community – the mosque helps to give a strong feeling to Muslims of being brothers and sisters together in the faith of Islam. It helps to bind the community together and adds to the cohesion of the community.

- An encouragement to faith – being together (and being seen together) gives Muslims encouragement to face up to the difficulties of living in a secular society. It helps them to resist all the pressures of living in a society that can often seem to be anti-religious and only interested in material pleasures.
- An opportunity to proclaim Islam – a mosque must seem like a beacon of Islam for many Muslims. Its distinctive design and features help to express the message of Islam and encourage Muslims to share their faith with others.

For discussion

How far can mosques help the Muslim community tell others about Islam? Give reasons for your viewpoint.

ResultsPlus
Build Better Answers

Do you think that money spent on building mosques would be better given to the poor?
Give **two** reasons for your point of view. (4 marks)

 Basic, 1-mark answers
These answers would give an opinion, but supported by one simple reason.

 Good, 2–3-mark answers
Good answers will support their opinion, with one developed and one simple reason.

 Excellent, 4-mark answers
Excellent answers will support their opinion with two developed reasons.

Summary

Mosques are places that give Muslims a sense of belonging. They are an important part of the community and offer numerous services to Muslims.

2.9 Reasons for differences between Sunni and Shi'ah communities

Learning outcomes

By the end of this lesson you should be able to:

- outline the main differences between Sunni and Shi'ah Muslims
- give your own opinion, with reasons, about these differences
- explain why there are differences between Sunni and Shi'ah Muslims
- evaluate different points of view about these differences, with reasons.

edexcel key terms

Shi'ah – Muslims who believe only the caliph Ali was rightly guided.

Sunni – Muslims who believe that the first four caliphs were rightly guided.

Activities

2 Do some research to find out in which countries Shi'ah Muslims are a large part of the population. Then make a chart of the information you have collected.

Athletes from Malaysia entering the Birds Nest Stadium in Beijing.

Activities

1 Look at the picture above of an Olympic opening ceremony. All the athletes look the same at the opening parade but we know that they all practise different sports. Discuss how you might find out the differences.

Religious communities that are made up of people from all over the world may hold their main beliefs in common but sometimes interpret history or understand an event in a variety of ways. Sometimes these differences are obvious, but often these differences only become clear when you talk to individuals.

How did the split happen?

The split between **Sunni** and **Shi'ah** Muslims goes back to the time immediately after the Prophet died. It was over the issue of who should lead the Muslim community after the death of Muhammad.

Sunni Muslims believe that Abu Bak'r was chosen by the community to be the successor to Muhammad. Leadership then passed to Umar, then to Uthman and lastly to Ali, the cousin and son-in-law of the Prophet. Sunni Muslims call these the 'four rightly guided Caliphs' (Khalifahs) or leaders.

Shi'ah Muslims believe that Ali was the Prophet's successor, that he was chosen and trained by the Prophet himself and that the leaders of the Muslim community would be descended from him. In other words, they would belong to the family line of the Prophet. The followers of Ali were called the party (shi'ah) of Ali.

The division between Sunni and Shi'ah Muslims continues to this day. About 85 per cent of all Muslims today are Sunni, and about 15 per cent are Shi'ah. In most countries, Sunni and Shi'ah live, work and worship Allah side by side, and co-operate when there is an issue important to all Muslims. In some parts of the world, sadly, there is deep division, conflict and sometimes violence between the two groups.

Similarities and differences

Things in common:

- They believe in Allah and His Prophet.
- They believe in the authority of the Qur'an.
- They believe in life after death and the judgement to follow.
- They both follow the Five Pillars.

Some of the issues on which the two groups are most deeply divided are shown in the following table.

There are also some different practices between the two groups:

- Saying the Shahadah – Shi'ahs may add 'and I bear witness that Ali was the friend of God'.
- The practice of salah – Shi'ahs prostrate the forehead onto earth or a small block of clay from Karbala.
- Important festivals and what they celebrate – Ashura, which commemorates the death of Husayn at Karbala, is the major mourning event for Shi'ahs.
- Places of pilgrimage – besides Makkah and Madinah, Shi'ahs also go to Karbala and Najaf.
- How much should be given to the poor – Shi'ahs also give 20 per cent of their savings called khums besides zakah.

All these practices centre around the importance of Ali and his descendents.

Issue	Sunni	Shi'ah	Reasons for Shi'ah belief
Person who leads the community	Four rightly guided Khalifahs, the first of whom Sunnis believe was chosen by the community	Twelve infallible Imams, the first of whom was Ali, the Prophet's cousin and son-in-law	Ali was appointed by Allah and declared by the Prophet on several occasions, the last being at Ghadir e Khum, after the final hajj
imam/Imam	Devout and knowledgeable Muslims who lead prayers (imams)	Spiritual guides chosen by Allah and given special knowledge; sinless (Imams)	Shi'ahs believe Ali and the Imams descended from him inherited the light of divine knowledge from Prophet Muhammad
Interpreting the Qur'an	Interpreted by knowledgeable scholars based on the traditions handed down	Interpreted by the Imams who have a special understanding of the Qur'an. This knowledge is passed on to scholars	Imams have divine guidance which gives them the infallible right to interpret the Qur'an

For discussion

Do you think differences between Sunni and Shi'ah Muslims matter?

Summary

The division between Sunni and Shi'ah Muslims began after the death of Muhammad, over who should be the right person to lead the community. The differences between them are not on matters of basic belief but on the importance of Ali as the successor to Muhammad.

2.10 The role and importance of groups and movements in British mosques

Learning outcomes

By the end of this lesson, you should be able to:

- outline the beliefs of some of the groups and movements that influence British mosques
- give your own opinion, with reasons, about the importance of these movements
- explain why different groups and movements are important in British mosques
- evaluate different points of view about the importance of these groups and movements, with reasons.

Other differences between Muslim groups

All religious groups have some people who believe everything in their religion must stay the same, and others who believe their religion must keep up with the times.

Here are some of the things Muslims differ about in this way:

- dress
- language
- culture
- roles of men and women
- how to deal with modern issues like abortion.

The main distinction in the Muslim community is between Sunni and Shi'ah Muslims. You explored some of the differences between these two groups on pages 48–49.

Other differences within both the Sunni and Shi'ah communities are likely to be found in many mosques. These differences in the Muslim community stem from other disagreements about what Muslims believe and how they should live. In the table opposite you will find reference to some of the groups within the Muslim community.

Activities

1 Look up the words 'traditionalist' and 'modernist' in a dictionary and write down the definitions.

Activities

2 Draw a table with four columns: in the first, list the things that Muslims hold differing opinions about. In the second, suggest what you think Muslim traditionalists would say or do about each issue. In the third, suggest what you think Muslim reformers would say or do about the same issues. In the last column, find out about any points on which they both agree. One row has been completed to get you started.

Subject of different opinion	Traditionalist view	Reformers' view	Points they would agree on
Dress	Traditional dress such as shalwar kameez	'Western' style of clothing	All dress should be 'modest'

Group	Distinguishing Features	Practices
Sunni – Barelvi	Revere the Prophet and seek his intercession	Chant the praises of the Prophet. Follow spiritual guidance of a Pir
Sunni – Deobandi	Consider the Prophet as an ordinary man and do not seek his intercession	Emphasis on removing anything considered as innovation, such as celebrating birthdays
Shi'ah Ithnasheri	Believe in the leadership of twelve Holy Imams or infallible spiritual guides after the Holy Prophet	Follow the guidance of jurists called Ayatollahs in daily life
Ismaili	Follow the Aga Khan as a spiritual leader	Worship in a Jamaatkhana and not a mosque. Have their own forms of worship and du'a instead of salah
Sufi	Emphasis on the spiritual rather than the physical	Use music and dance as forms of worship

Although there are these different groups within the world-wide community of Muslims, it is important to remember that they are still all Muslims who believe the greatness and oneness of Allah – tawhid. They all follow the teaching of the Qur'an and seek to follow the straight path laid down by Allah. The differences may define certain practices but it is this common goal of living a life in obedience to Allah – that is the most important part of their belief.

Activities

Challenge

3   Do some research to find out if there are different Muslim groups in your area and then see if you can identify what the differences might be.

4   In pairs discuss how important is it for all the members of one religion to believe and practice exactly the same things.

5   Find out about the Ahmadiyya movement. What do the members believe that is different from other Muslim groups? How are they regarded by other Muslims?

Summary

Like all religions, Islam contains believers who have different points of view upon many issues. This has caused different groups and movements to form in some mosques.

2.11 Different attitudes to Sufi forms of worship

52

Learning outcomes

By the end of this lesson, you should be able to:

- outline Sufi forms of worship
- give your own opinion, with reasons, about these forms of worship
- explain why there are different attitudes among Muslims to Sufi forms of worship
- evaluate different points of view about these attitudes, with reasons.

Activities

1. Find out what the word 'sufi' means and where the word comes from. What does the meaning tell you about who the Sufis are?

Sufi worship

The name 'Sufi' refers to a number of Muslim groups, organisations and movements who all have some common ideas and practices. They all aim to help Muslims to become closer to Allah in their faith, their worship and their daily lives. Sufis believe that the most important thing in life is to be close to Allah in their love for Him and in their devotion to Him. To help them to do this, they:

- try to live a simple life
- avoid attachment to material possessions
- try to overcome their own selfishness
- concentrate on Allah.

These ideas are shared by most Muslims. However, some groups of Sufis go further in their devotions and practise rituals that other Muslims dislike. These include the use of music and dancing, which Sufis believe bring them closer to Allah, so that the rhythm of the music and the regular movement of the dance take them 'out of themselves' and into a state where their mind is fixed on Allah alone.

Sufi dancers sometimes called 'whirling dervishes'.

Sufis often use music to help them worship.

Different attitudes to Sufism

Sufis believe that the purpose of worship is to become so close to Allah that the worshipper, in a sense, becomes part of Allah, joined to Allah or united with Allah.

- They say that their approach to the Muslim way of life is very close to that of the Prophet himself.
- They believe their way avoids simply following the rules of religion and the formal rituals of the Five Pillars for their own sake and helps them to concentrate on the inward and spiritual life that brings them closer to Allah.

Some other Muslims are deeply concerned that this kind of worship is dangerous and that Allah has defined how He should be worshipped through the Five Pillars. Only by following the rules of the Shari'ah and keeping to the rituals set out in the Five Pillars can a person live a life that is pleasing to Allah. Many Muslims believe that all music is forbidden by the Qur'an and hadith. Others believe that instruments are forbidden but singing is allowed.

Results**Plus**
Build Better Answers

Explain why there are different attitudes to Sufi forms of worship. (8 marks)

■ **Basic, 1–2-mark answers**

Basic answers usually describe Sufi worship rather than giving reasons why there are different attitudes to it.

● **Good, 3–6-mark answers**

Good answers tend to give two reasons without any development. These answers can be further improved by explaining the reasons given or by giving more of them.

▲ **Excellent, 7–8-mark answers**

Most excellent answers will give four reasons. Other excellent answers will give fewer reasons but develop them. It is possible to write an excellent answer by giving just one reason, but this would need to be explained in real depth.

Summary

'Sufi' refers to certain Islamic groups. Sufis believe that becoming closer to Allah is the most important thing and some groups use controversial ways of worshipping, such as chanting, music and dance.

KnowZone
Community and tradition

Quick quiz

1 Give four ways in which Muslims show respect for the Qur'an.

2 What is an imam?

3 Name four features of a mosque.

4 Give two differences between Sunnis and Shi'ahs.

5 What is meant by 'Shari'ah'?

6 Give four examples of things an imam might do.

7 Give four activities that take place in mosques.

8 What is the most important reason why the Qur'an has supreme authority for Muslims?

9 What is meant by 'ummah'?

10 Give an example of a Sufi form of worship.

Find out more

You could develop your knowledge about all the topics in this section by visiting your local mosque or asking someone from the mosque to visit your class. There are also a number of good websites to help you, such as the BBC Religion and Ethics website – you can go to www.pearsonhotlinks.co.uk (express code 4264P) and click on the 'Find out more about Islam' link. It is essential that you understand how important these topics are for Muslims.

Plenary activity

Prepare an e-mail to a Muslim group with a series of questions that you would like answered about the mosque and its role in your local community.

Self-evaluation checklist

How well have you understood the topics in this section? In the first column of the table below use the following code to rate your understanding:

Green – I understand this fully

Orange – I am confident I can answer most questions on this.

Red – I need to do a lot more work on this topic.

In the second and third columns you need to think about:

● whether you have an opinion on this topic and could give reasons for that opinion, if asked.

● whether you can give the opinion of someone who disagrees with you and give reasons for this alternative opinion.

Content covered	My understanding is red/orange/ green	Can I give my opinion?	Can I give an alternative opinion?
● The meaning of Muhammad as the Seal of the Prophets			
● Why belief in Muhammad as the Seal of the Prophets is important to Muslims			
● Why the Qur'an has supreme authority for Muslims			
● How Muslims show respect for the Qur'an			
● Why Muslims show respect for the Qur'an			
● Why the ummah is important for Muslims			
● The main features and purposes of a mosque			
● The role of the imam in a mosque			
● Why the imam is important			
● The role of the mosque for the local Muslim community			
● Why the mosque is important for the local Muslim community			
● Reasons for the differences between Sunni and Shi'ah communities			
● The meaning and importance of different groups and movements in British mosques			
● Different attitudes to Sufi forms of worship			

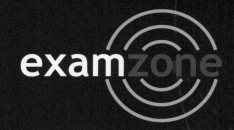

Introduction

In the exam you will see a choice of two questions on this module. Each question will include four tasks, which test your knowledge, understanding and evaluation of the material covered. A 2-mark question will ask you to define a term; a 4-mark question will ask your opinion on a point of view; an 8-mark question will ask you to explain a particular belief or idea; a 6-mark question will ask for your opinion on a point of view and ask you to consider an alternative point of view.

You must give your opinion, but also include the reasons for your opinion. You should give two reasons – any more than this and you will be wasting valuable time.

Mini exam paper

(a) What is **bismillah**? (2 marks)

(b) Do you think mosques are important for the Muslim community?

Give **two** reasons for your point of view. (4 marks)

(c) Explain why the ummah is important for Muslims. (8 marks)

(d) 'The Qur'an is the only authority for Muslims.'

In your answer you should refer to Islam.

(i) Do you agree? Give reasons for your opinion. (3 marks)

(ii) Give reasons why some people may disagree with you. (3 marks)

Give a glossary definition. You do not need to write any more – often this can be done in one sentence.

This question is worth the most so it is important that you spend some time on it. 'Explain why' means that you need to give reasons. A good answer here will often give four reasons, but you could give fewer reasons and still produce a good response if you develop them. This is also the question where you should double-check the quality of your spelling and punctuation. Remember to take care when writing your answers, and to use proper sentences and not bullet points.

This question is always split into two parts and you should answer each part separately. For at least one of the parts you must refer to Muslim beliefs, and it's probably a good idea to consider what Muslims think first and then either use that for your own opinion or for the alternative opinion in (ii).

Mark scheme

(a) You will earn **2 marks** for a correct answer, and **1 mark** for a partially correct answer.

(b) To earn up to the full **4 marks** you need to give two reasons (as asked) and develop them. Two brief reasons or one developed reason will earn **2 marks** and one reason without development will earn **1 mark**.

(c) You can earn **7–8 marks** by giving up to four reasons, but the fewer reasons you give, the more you must develop them. You are being assessed on your use of language, so you also need to take care to express your understanding in a clear style of English and make some use of specialist vocabulary.

(d) To go beyond **3 marks** for the whole of this question you must refer to Islam. The more you are able to develop your reasons the more marks you will earn. Three simple reasons can earn you the same mark as one developed reason.

ResultsPlus
Build Better Answers

(c) Explain why the ummah is important for Muslims. (8 marks)

Student answer	Comments	Improved student answer
The ummah is made up of all Muslims everywhere. It does not matter about your race or your sex, you are part of the ummah. The ummah is very important to Muslims and is shown in the way they all do the same things on hajj. Muhammad said that the ummah was like a building with all the parts supporting each other. This is important because all Muslims should work together to help each other.	This answer has made statements that, although they are correct, do not answer the question of *why* the ummah is important. Except for the last sentence they only describe the ummah.	The ummah is made up of all Muslims everywhere. It does not matter about your race or your sex, you are part of the ummah. This is important because Muslims believe that all human beings were made by Allah and are equal, and this is shown in the idea of ummah or brotherhood. Muhammad said that the ummah was like a building with all the parts supporting each other. This gives Muslims a feeling of belonging to the community whether they are rich or poor. This is important because all Muslims should work together to help each other and support each other as members of one family. The ummah is also important because it is based on the idea of unity and the oneness of Allah.

Worship and celebration

Introduction

In this section you will learn about the obligatory acts of worship that help Muslims to keep in contact with Allah, strengthen their faith and reinforce the ummah. These are called the Five Pillars because they support the key beliefs of Muslims.

You will also reflect upon the significance of these acts for Muslims and be able to evaluate their importance in the daily life of a Muslim.

Worship is based on the feeling that there is something or someone that is greater than you. Muslims worship Allah because Allah is great. 'Allahu Akbar' ('God is great') begins the call to prayer and so Muslims are constantly reminded to worship Allah.

The Qur'anic word for worship is 'ibadah', which comes from the Arabic word for 'to serve'. So, for Muslims, to worship Allah is the same as to serve Allah. Every aspect of life, both rest and work, is focused on Allah the Creator and all-powerful god. Ibadah is not about just going to the mosque or saying salah, it is doing everything with an awareness that Allah is everywhere.

Learning outcomes for this section

By the end of this section you should be able to:

- give definitions of the key terms and use them in answer to GCSE questions
- explain the meaning of each of the Five Pillars
- express an opinion, with reasons, about the significance of the Five Pillars to a Muslim
- evaluate different points of view, giving reasons.

edexcel ⣿ key terms

Arafat	qiblah	Shahadah
hajj	Ramadan	tawaf
Id-ul-Adha	salah	wudu
Id-ul-Fitr	sawm	zakah

Fascinating fact

Islam is the second-largest religion in the world with over 1 billion followers. In 2009, more than 2 million Muslims went on hajj to Makkah.

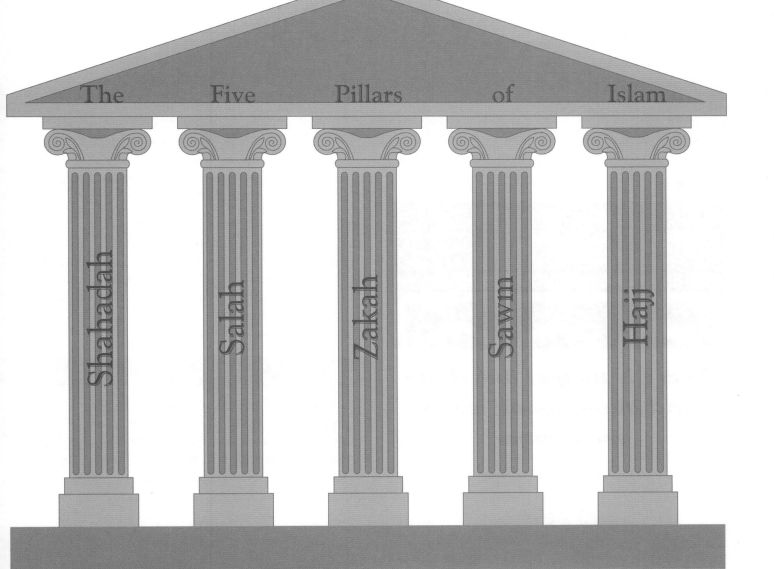

In pairs, using the key terms as the basis of your work, draw a diagram showing how the Five Pillars link together and then add to your diagram any other information that you know, for example how often a Muslim must do salah.

3.1 The meaning and significance of the Shahadah as a summary of Islamic belief

60

Learning outcomes

By the end of this lesson, you should be able to:

● know and explain what the Shahadah is

● give reasons why reciting the Shahadah is important to a Muslim

● evaluate the significance of the Shahadah to a Muslim.

edexcel ▦ key terms

Shahadah – The declaration of faith in Allah and His Prophet.

What is the Shahadah?

There is no god but Allah and Muhammad is His messenger

This statement is the Shahadah and it supports the other pillars.

For a person to recite these words and mean them is to declare themselves a Muslim. They are saying that they belong to the Islamic faith.

Everyone likes to feel they belong to something. In our lives we all belong to different groups. Sometimes we are born into a group and sometimes we choose to join one. Some groups have a uniform for members to wear, other groups have a badge and some have a statement to recite or sign. All these things help to show who belongs and who does not.

Activities

1 Make a list of groups to which you belong, for example your family. Next to the name of the group write down anything you do or have that shows that you belong to that group, for example your surname shows you belong to your family.

Most religions have a creed (statement of belief) that people accept if they belong to the religion. This creed will contain the most important beliefs of the religion.

For a Muslim the **Shahadah** is a very important statement as it sums up what one must believe to be a Muslim.

The Shahadah starts with the words *'There is no god but Allah'*. This is tawhid, which you will have studied in Section 1 (see pages 2–25).

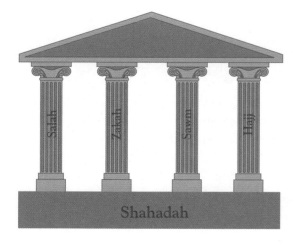

Without this belief there would not be a religion called Islam. This belief helps Muslims live their lives with confidence, knowing that there is an All-Powerful being in control of the world. Man has a role to play, which is set down for him in the Qur'an. For a Muslim the best example of how to live and fulfil this role is shown in the life of the Prophet Muhammad. This is summarised in the second part of the Shahadah: '…*Muhammad is the messenger of Allah*'.

Why is the Shahadah significant in the life of a Muslim?

This declaration sums up all Muslim belief. The bubbles below show how and when it is used.

repeated in Salah

keep saying it throughout the day

last words you hear or say before death

recited in the adhan (call to prayer)

whisper it to a newborn baby

teach it to children

Activities

2 In pairs discuss how repeating the Shahadah throughout the day might help a Muslim follow the teachings of Islam.

By declaring the Shahadah a Muslim is saying the following:

1 There is no room in their life for any god except Allah. This is a very difficult statement to make and keep, but for a Muslim it is absolutely crucial if they are to live a good Islamic life. Announcing the absoluteness of Allah, the All-Powerful, All-Knowing being, means that one must submit to Allah and obey His commands. Nothing less than complete obedience is good enough for such a great god.

2 The belief in Muhammad as the messenger of Allah is accepting that Islam, as given directly to the Prophet by Allah, is the final and complete guidance of Allah for humans. It is also a statement where one is declaring the intention to follow that guidance in every part of life. This could be difficult

in a world where there are many other things that seem important; everybody needs help to live a good life. For Muslims, following the example of the Prophet Muhammad is the best way to ensure that the will of Allah is the centre of their life.

The Shahadah is very brief but it is fundamental to a Muslim's whole way of life because:

• Muslims believe that the purpose of life for human beings is to worship Allah alone. Every day and each minute of a Muslim's life should be spent in worship of Allah. The commitment made by the first recitation of the Shahadah is renewed by constant repetition throughout the day.

• A Muslim performs every act in the name of and to obtain the pleasure of Allah. This is ibadah (see pages 6–7). Worshipping Allah means serving Allah, and everything that a Muslim does during the day is motivated by this idea. This means everything must be done to the very best of one's ability.

• Allah gave humans life and they have a responsibility to live it in the way Allah intended. The only way a Muslim can do this is to follow the Qur'an and the example of Muhammad.

Activities

3 Think of about ten activities you do during the week and make up a questionnaire to find out how these activities might be done in a Muslim way to show worship of Allah. Then ask your family and friends to complete the questionnaire.

For discussion

To what extent do you think reciting a statement of faith can make someone a member of a religion? In groups discuss this question and produce a document outlining the arguments for and against this question. You should use examples and give reasons for the different points of view.

Summary

The Shahadah is the declaration of faith that anyone becoming a Muslim must make. It is the first pillar of Islam and the foundation on which the other pillars are based.

3.2 The practice and significance of salah

Learning outcomes

By the end of this lesson, you should be able to:

● define the key terms

● explain how and why Muslims practise salah

● give reasons for the importance of salah in the life of a Muslim

● give an opinion, with reasons, about the significance of salah.

What is salah?

How do you get to know your friends, your teachers, even your family? You talk to them and listen to them so that you know what things they like and what they do not like. This helps you to understand the best way of being friends and enjoying each other's company. So how do Muslims get to know God?

In Islam there are five compulsory daily prayers. This is called **salah** and is the second pillar of Islam.

edexcel ::: key terms

salah – The five daily prayers.

wudu – The washing that must take place before salah.

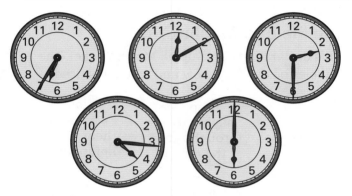

Muslims offer salah because:

● it is commanded in the Qur'an: *'Establish regular prayers – at the sun's decline till the darkness of the night, and the recital of the Qur'an for the recital of the Qur'an at dawn is witnessed.'* (Surah 17:78)

● they must remember Allah throughout the day and prayer helps them do this

● it makes them feel closer to Allah

● it unites them with other Muslims

● it reconfirms their faith.

The practice of salah

Salah is very sacred (holy) as it is when a Muslim seeks to come into direct contact with Allah. Therefore, before saying salah, Muslims must prepare themselves by making **wudu**. Wudu is ritual washing. There are a number of rules for salah:

1 Perform wudu.

2 Pray five times a day at set times.

3 Face Makkah.

4 Perform certain actions – standing, bowing, prostrating and sitting. These must be repeated in a certain order and a certain number of times.

5 Recite in Arabic.

During salah Muslims praise Allah and recite verses from the Qur'an. They do not ask Allah for things during salah. Muslims must pray at the set times wherever they may be, whether it is a mosque, at home, at work or at school. They may combine the timings of the two afternoon prayers and the two evening prayers if there is difficulty in praying five times a day. So they would pray five prayers at three times: morning, midday and evening.

The place of prayer is not important, but it must be clean. Many Muslims will carry a prayer mat with them so that they can be sure the place they are using is clean. Whenever possible it is best to pray with other Muslims and be united in the worship of Allah. On Friday midday, as far as possible, all adult males must take part in the Jum'ah prayers at the mosque. This means a Muslim must keep very strict discipline in their life if they are to follow the rules exactly, but keeping these rules helps them to remember Allah at all times of the day and focus their life on Him.

The significance of salah to a Muslim

Salah is considered by many Muslims to be the most important of the practical pillars (salah, sawm, zakah and hajj). It is a way of showing total submission to Allah, seeking his forgiveness, but is also a way of identifying with the worldwide community of Islam.

What are these positions stating?

We all forget to do things, for instance perhaps we forget a person's birthday. It is useful to have something to remind us of things. Muslims believe that because salah constantly punctuates their day it helps them to remember Allah. Therefore, not only does it remind them of Allah's greatness, but also it improves their behaviour, which will bring rewards. Allah says in the Qur'an *'Then do you remember Me; I will remember you…'* (Surah 2:152).

For a Muslim to gain most benefit from salah, the intention – niyyah – must be right. Just saying words without meaning is meaningless. The heart must be involved in the actions. In addition to the set prayers, Muslims also perform du'a – the prayer of the heart. This can be done at any time and is often done after completing the salah.

For discussion

Reflect on the idea of niyyah – intention. Can you think of any evidence that might show if a person is really performing salah in the way Allah intended?

Summary

Salah is the second pillar of Islam. It is the five daily prayers that Muslims must perform. It is seen as very significant because it helps Muslims to focus on Allah and brings them closer to Allah.

3.3 The practice and significance of zakah

64

edexcel ⠿ key terms

zakah – A tax Muslims must pay for the poor.

Activities

1   Can you imagine being Bill Gates, the billionaire owner of Microsoft? What might you spend a great deal of your time thinking about? In pairs make a list of things you think might worry you, if you were Bill Gates. How many of these are about money or belongings?

What is zakah?

We all need money in order to live in today's world and clearly some people have more than others.

Muslims believe that:

- all men and all things were made by Allah and belong to Allah
- everything humans have is on loan and must be looked after carefully as, in the life after death, Allah will judge how each person has used the gifts Allah has given them
- part of the responsibility of each individual is to share whatever they have with other people.

Zakah is the third pillar of Islam. It is giving money to be used for the poor.

The meaning of the word zakah is 'to purify', so this giving of money to help others is to 'cleanse' you of too much desire or greed for your money and possessions. The idea is that, by giving this money, you learn not to place too much importance on material wealth (cash and possessions). This is very important for Muslims because they believe that everything they own has been given to them by Allah.

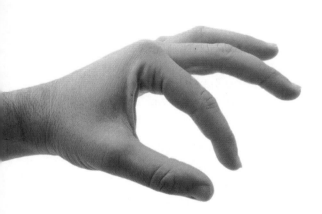

Zakah is not an option, it is a compulsory act for all Muslims. It is written in the Qur'an and is a direct command from Allah. It is often linked with prayer and is part of a Muslim's worship of Allah.

In practice, it is a contribution of money paid once a year of 2.5 per cent based on how much one has in savings, cash and jewellery. It is paid to the mosque, in secret, as only Allah has the right to judge whether a person is giving sufficiently.

Although zakah is often defined as a tax, it is different from a tax because it cannot be used by the government for general purposes. In many Islamic states the collection and distribution of zakah is undertaken by the government. Generally in non-Islamic states the mosque committee will decide how the money will be used. However, many Muslims undertake the responsibility themselves and might give their zakah to a recognised charity or people they know who are in need.

Zakah can only be used for certain things:

- helping the poor
- helping people in need
- freeing prisoners
- helping people out of debt.

These guidelines are set out in the Qur'an in Surah 9. These uses can be understood to include building mosques or Islamic schools.

For a Muslim, zakah of 2.5 per cent is the absolute minimum that is required as a religious duty from those who possess wealth. It is not the maximum. Islam encourages everyone to give as much as they can in charity. Most Muslims also give sadaqah, which is a voluntary gift made out of love in order to seek the pleasure of God.

In Surah 2:264 Allah says, '… *Cancel not your charity by reminders of your generosity or by injury – like those who spend their wealth to be seen of men, but believe in neither Allah nor in the Last Day. They are in parable like a hard, barren rock, on which is a little soil: on it falls heavy rain, which leaves it (just) a bare stone…*'

Why is zakah significant in the life of a Muslim?

Muslims believe that they have been given the responsibility for caring for Allah's creation and using the resources Allah has provided to help humanity in the best way possible. Generosity is always encouraged in Islam and is part of the process of becoming less self-centred and more focused on Allah. This is called 'taqwa' or 'God-consciousness'.

Here are some reasons why Muslims believe that giving zakah is important:

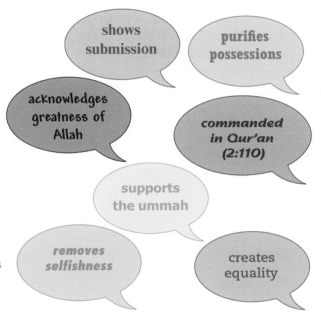

shows submission

purifies possessions

acknowledges greatness of Allah

commanded in Qur'an (2:110)

supports the ummah

removes selfishness

creates equality

Activities

2 Which of the above statements do you think are the most important reasons for giving zakah? Explain your choices.

Summary

Zakah is the third pillar of Islam. It is the compulsory donation given by Muslims to help the poor. It is significant because it helps Muslims to remember that material wealth is a gift entrusted to them by Allah and must be shared.

For discussion

Read the verse above very carefully. With a partner discuss what this might mean about how zakah should be given.

3.4 The relationship of zakah to the ummah

Learning outcomes

By the end of this lesson, you should be able to:

- understand the relationship between zakah and the ummah
- explain why giving zakah is important to the ummah for Muslims
- evaluate, with reasons, the value of zakah to the worldwide community of Muslims.

A fundamental belief of Islam is that Allah created all humans and everybody must be treated equally, regardless of race or colour. It does not matter where you live in the world, which football team you support or whether you are rich or poor, everyone is equal in the sight of Allah.

Within the human race there are groups of people who possess the same beliefs and values and naturally feel closer to each other, like members of a family, because they are enjoying the same interests.

Many groups, like members of a family, will look out for each other and give help when needed.

All Muslims are part of the worldwide group or religion known as Islam. In Islam the idea of the community of believers – known as the ummah (see pages 40–41) – is very important.

The Prophet said that believers are like the parts of a building as each part supports the others.

It is this idea of all belonging to one another and depending on one another that is very important to Muslims. It does not matter who you are or where you live – it is the fact that you are a Muslim that makes you a member of the ummah.

Why is zakah important for the ummah?

Remember, zakah is giving a part of your wealth to help others in need (pages 64–65).

As the members of the ummah live in both rich and poor countries it is the duty of every Muslim who is able to help, to give charity to those who are in need.

Activities

1 Make a list of the different groups that you belong to and write next to each one what sort of people also belong to it. Think about each group and where possible make a note of where you think the group gets money in order to run. The table below will help you:

Group	Members of group	How is group funded?
family	parents, children, grandparents	parents' work
sports club	players, coach	
school		

In Muslim society, people sharing their wealth in this way is a form of social security. One person sharing their wealth with others helps the whole world community to live well together. Allah has commanded that members of the ummah should care for each other, so giving zakah is not a choice but an act of faith and worship.

Muslims believe that Allah decides who will be rich, who will be poor and who will live, who will die. They also believe that they have a duty to care for the poor and give zakah in order to redress the balance between rich and poor. The effectiveness of the ummah is strengthened by sharing resources.

For discussion

Why doesn't Allah just give everyone equal amounts?

Muslims have a duty to help others who are in need. Muhammad taught that whoever eats his fill while his neighbour remains hungry is not a believer and that giving zakah reminds one that rich and poor are all members of the ummah.

'And be steadfast in prayer; practise regular charity…' (Surah 2:43) – everyone obeying Allah's commands unites the ummah and demonstrates an act of faith.

Why is zakah important for the ummah?

Knowing that all Muslims are giving zakah at the same time, to be used for the same purposes, brings unity with other Muslims.

Sharing resources strengthens the ummah and helps people gain spiritual riches.

Muslims live in most countries of the world. Many of those countries are very poor.

Activities

2 Debate the issue: 'Governments should care for the poor.'

3 Do some research to find some of the ways that zakah is used to strengthen the ummah around the world.

Summary

Muslims worldwide, both rich and poor, are members of the ummah. Giving zakah makes the ummah stronger because it encourages each person to consider the needs of others and reminds them that they are brothers and sisters in the sight of Allah.

3.5 The practice and significance of sawm during Ramadan

edexcel ⠿ key terms

Ramadan – The ninth month when the Qur'an says all Muslims must fast.

sawm – Fasting by going without food and drink during daylight hours.

What is sawm?

Have you seen starving children? Have you ever been really hungry? Perhaps you have tried or been sponsored to give up a favourite food to raise money for charity.

Activities

1 Try writing down how you felt when you looked at the picture above.

'Fasting' means to go without food. **Sawm** is fasting during the month of **Ramadan**. For Muslims to fast during the month of Ramadan they must abstain from food and drink during the hours of daylight – from dawn to dusk.

Sawm is the fourth pillar of Islam and is another act of ibadah.

Sawm helps the Muslim to remain truly obedient to Allah's commands. The Qur'an says:

> 'O you who believe! Fasting is prescribed to you as it was prescribed to those before you, that you may (learn) self-restraint.' (Surah 2:183)

In the Qur'an, Allah says that fasting should begin when *'the white streak of dawn appear[s] to you distinct from the blackness of night'* (Surah 2:187).

Sawm in Ramadan means, during daylight hours:

- No food or drink of any sort. This means not even having a sip of water after P.E. lessons at school or after a game of football.

- No smoking, including passive smoking. This means being very careful where you go so that you avoid other people smoking.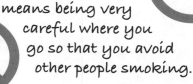

- No sexual activity

- Making an extra effort to avoid bad thoughts and deeds. You should not tell a lie or break a promise.

Not all Muslims are expected to fast. Those who do not have to fast include:

- those who are physically or mentally unwell
- children who have not reached puberty
- the very old
- those who are pregnant or breast-feeding
- those who are travelling.

If an adult does not fast for any one of the reasons above, they should try to make up the fast at a later date, or make a donation to the poor instead.

When daylight is over most Muslims will break or open the fast with dates or water, following the example of the Prophet Muhammad, before having a proper meal later. Because Ramadan is a time to spend with friends and family, the fast will often be broken by families coming together to share in an evening meal.

Muhammad broke his fast with a handful of dates.

The very purpose of fasting is to make a Muslim able to control their feelings and thoughts, so that they become a person of good deeds and intentions.

Why is observing sawm during Ramadan significant for Muslims?

Ramadan is the ninth and holiest month of the Islamic lunar calendar.

During Ramadan the Night of Power occurs. It is the holiest night of the holiest month because it is believed to be the night on which God first began revealing the Qur'an to the Prophet Muhammad through the Angel Jibril (Gabriel). This is a time for especially fervent and devoted prayer, and there are many rewards and blessings associated with remembering this time.

Muslims are told in the Qur'an that praying throughout this one night is better than a thousand months of prayer. Whoever spends this night in prayer with faith, hoping for Allah's reward, will have all his past sins forgiven. The Prophet is reported to have said that at the start of the month of Ramadan the gates of Paradise are opened, the gates of Hell are closed and devils are put in chains.

No one knows exactly which night it is but hadith indicate it is one of the odd nights in the last ten nights of the month. Therefore Muslims will dedicate these nights in extra worship and prayer and also try to recite the whole Qur'an in one month – 1/30 on each night.

Sawm is commanded in the Qur'an. It is an act of deeply personal worship in which Muslims seek a raised level of God-consciousness – taqwa.

For discussion

'If fasting and spending the Night of Power in prayer, during Ramadan, is worth a thousand months of prayer, then it wouldn't matter if a Muslim forgot salah now and again.'

Summary

Ramadan is the holiest month of the year because it contains the Night of Power. Fasting and prayer during this month unite the community in thought for others and focuses a Muslim on self-purification and seeking forgiveness from God.

3.6 The reasons for and benefits of fasting

70

Why do Muslims fast?

Muslims can fast at any time of the year for a long time or a short time. The purpose of fasting is to focus on self-purification and spend more time in prayer and worship of Allah.

However, most Muslims concentrate their fasting during the month of Ramadan for a number of reasons:

- It is commanded in the Qur'an (2:185).
- It encourages fellowship with other Muslims through the shared experience of fasting at the same time.
- It is a special time to give thanks for the Holy Qur'an, which was first revealed in the month of Ramadan.
- Fasting is not just a physical experience but is rather the total commitment of the person's body and soul to the spirit of the fast and is seen as a method of self-purification as well as self-control. Purity of thought and action is most important.

Muslims all over the world fast during Ramadan, but the length of the day will be different depending on where in the world they live. Fasting becomes especially difficult in countries far from the equator in summer, when daylight may last 18 hours. Can you imagine how hard it would be to go without food or water for 18 hours every day for 30 days?

What are the benefits of fasting?

Fasting is like a pathway that brings the Muslim closer to Allah.

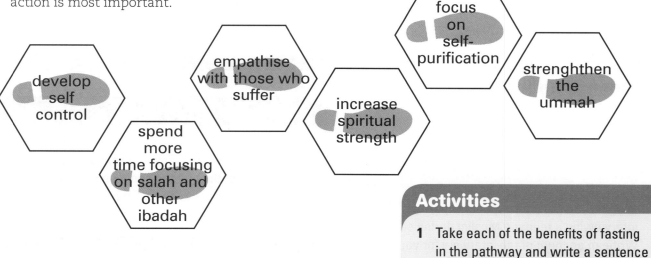

Muslims are encouraged to read the Qur'an and perform special prayers, called Taraweh, which are held in the mosques every night of the month. Over Ramadan the whole of the Qur'an can be recited in these prayers. The month of Ramadan is a time for spiritual reflection, prayer, doing good deeds and spending time with family and friends. During the month of Ramadan people make a special effort to come together and break their fast after dark. Sharing food with neighbours and eating together as a family gives everyone more time to spend together.

Breaking fast together at the end of each day of Ramadan brings Muslim communities closer together.

A truly obedient Muslim is called a Muttaqi and his true obedience or piety – developed through sawm – is known as taqwa in Islam. taqwa keeps a person away from sin. During Ramadan Muslims believe that Satan is locked up in order to help them increase their taqwa and avoid evil.

For discussion

- What do you think would be the most difficult things about fasting?
- What do you think would be the best things about fasting?

Build Better Answers

Explain how sawm (fasting) can bring benefits to Muslims. (8 marks)

■ Basic, 1–2-mark answers

Basic answers usually describe sawm rather than giving examples of the benefits it can bring to Muslims.

● Good, 3–6-mark answers

Level two answers (3–4 marks) tend to give two benefits without any development. Level three answers (5–6 marks) will explain the benefits.

▲ Excellent, 7–8-mark answers

Most excellent answers will give four benefits that sawm can bring to Muslims. Other excellent answers will give fewer benefits but explain them. It is possible to get full marks by giving just one benefit, but this would need to be explained in real depth.

Summary

Most Muslims fast because it is commanded in the Qur'an, as it gives them an opportunity to give thanks for the Holy Qur'an and because it brings the ummah together. It also brings many benefits to Muslims, such as increasing their awareness of the suffering of others and becoming more spiritual and closer to Allah.

3.7 The meaning and significance of the celebration of Id-ul-Fitr

Learning outcomes

By the end of this lesson, you should be able to:

- explain what Id-ul-Fitr is and how it is celebrated
- understand why Muslims celebrate Id-ul-Fitr
- express an opinion, with reasons, about how significant this festival is to a Muslim

edexcel ⠿ key terms

Id-ul-Fitr – The festival of breaking the fast.

Activities

1 Think of the special occasions you celebrate during the year. Choose one and describe it to the rest of the class. Include why it is special, what you do, what you eat and who you celebrate with.

What is Id-ul-Fitr?

The end of Ramadan is marked by a three-day period known as **Id-ul-Fitr,** the 'Festival of breaking the fast'. This Id is known as the 'small' festival as it lasts only three days.

'Id' is an Arabic word meaning something that keeps happening, and in Islam it is used for the religious festivals. 'Fitr' means 'to break', and this particular festival marks the breaking of the fasting period of Ramadan. It can also signify the break-up of bad deeds as a result of increased self-control.

When the first crescent of the new moon has been officially sighted by a reliable source, the month of Ramadan and the fast is declared over, and the month of Shawwal begins.

When Ramadan ends, Muslims give to charity in a locally prescribed amount, calculated to feed one poor person in that region for one day. This is known as 'zakat al fitra', and is meant as another reminder of the suffering endured by many.

Many Muslims also take this occasion to pay the annual alms that are due to the poor and needy, known as zakah (see pages 64–65).

At the start of Id everyone comes together and says a special prayer. My mum and I decorate our hands with Mehndi patterns. These are reddish-brown colour and look like leaves or swirling shapes. Lots of women do this for Id.

I love Id, it's my favourite festival. Everyone dresses up, decorates their homes and has fun. Many people give presents, especially to children.

At the beginning of Ramadan, it is appropriate to wish Muslims 'Ramadan Mubarak', which means 'Blessed Ramadan'. At its conclusion, you may say, 'Id Mubarak'.

Muslims are not only celebrating the end of fasting, but thanking Allah for the help and strength that He gave them throughout the previous month to help them practise self-control.

There are special services out of doors and in mosques, processions through the streets and, of course, a special celebratory meal – eaten during daytime, the first daytime meal Muslims will have had in a month.

The tradition of having the Id prayer in the open, in a field or some similar place, sums up the beauty and simplicity of Id: standing together – all equal, praising the Creator.

Id celebrations in Trafalgar Square.

Why is it important to celebrate Id-ul-Fitr?

Muslims do not have many festivals, so why is there a festival at the end of the month-long fast during Ramadan?

This festival is not about remembering a great event from the past but is a sign of gratefulness by Muslims on completing Ramadan, and as a celebration for those who spent the month of Ramadan in fasting and performing other forms of ibadah. This also reminds Muslims that they should not rely only on what people have done in the past, but that they must themselves focus on good acts in order to please Allah.

- Id is also a time of forgiveness, and for making amends.
- Id unites human beings in common joy. It reminds a Muslim of the importance of harmony, human equality and compassion for all.
- Id is also a time for giving and sharing, and allows Muslims the opportunity to reflect on their duty to help people who are less fortunate than themselves.
- Id is the time for Muslims to appreciate their family, their friends and their responsibilities to the community of which they all are a part.

It is said that every day in which a Muslim does not disobey Allah is a day of Id.

Activities

2 Look at the picture of the celebrations of Id above. Write a short paragraph explaining why it is important for Muslims (a) to celebrate Id together and (b) to celebrate in the open air.

Watch out!

Many students get confused between Id-ul-Fitr and Id-ul-Adha. Make sure that you know the differences between them!

Activities

3 Write down at least two ways that Id-ul-Fitr brings Muslims closer together (a) as families and (b) as the ummah.

Summary

Id-ul-Fitr is the festival celebrated to break the fast at the end of Ramadan. It is a time to be spent with families and for the ummah to praise Allah.

3.8 The meaning and significance of the events of hajj in Makkah (1)

Learning outcomes

By the end of this lesson, you should be able to:

- explain the importance of hajj to Muslims
- evaluate the significance of hajj
- know what happens in Makkah
- understand the importance of going to Makkah for a Muslim
- give an opinion, with reasons, about how seeing the Ka'bah makes a difference to a Muslim.

edexcel key terms

hajj – The annual pilgrimage to Makkah.

What is hajj?

Hajj is the fifth and final pillar of Islam. It is the pilgrimage to Makkah.

Is there somewhere in the world that you would really like to visit? Perhaps there is a country or a city that you have read about and it looks very interesting. Perhaps there is somewhere that you have already been that is a special place for you and you want to go back there. Sometimes it is just exciting to go on a journey and visit somewhere new.

Makkah in Saudi Arabia is a very special place for Muslims because it was there that the Prophet Muhammad was born and where he received the very first revelation from Allah. All Muslims want to visit Makkah at least once in their lifetime.

Hajj occurs in the month of Dhul Hijjah, which is the twelfth month of the Islamic lunar calendar. Hajj is a journey that every sane, adult Muslim must undertake at least once in their lives if they can afford it and are physically able. Many Muslims save for years in order to perform the pilgrimage. They often have to travel thousands of miles. Pilgrims generally travel on hajj in groups.

Hajj is the worldwide gathering of the family of Islam in an act of worship, regardless of social status, wealth, nationality or colour.

The pilgrimage enables Muslims from all around the world, of different colours, languages, races and ethnicities, to come together in a spirit of universal brotherhood and sisterhood to worship the One God together.

Activities

1 There are many things that pilgrims do and experience that show they are all equal. Begin a chart with two columns. List the action and then write down how it shows equality.

2 Prepare a brochure advertising a journey to Makkah for hajj. Include in it approximate cost, length of journey, basic necessities, etc. There are many websites to help you.

During hajj, male pilgrims are required to dress only in a garment consisting of two sheets of white unhemmed cloth. Women are simply required to maintain their hijab (see pages 100–101) and normal modest dress, which does not cover the hands or face. These simple garments, known as the ihram clothing, strip away distinctions of class and culture and symbolise the fact that all stand equal before Allah, whether rich or poor.

Ihram also symbolises leaving behind all worldly possessions and worries in order to return to God.

A pilgrim concentrates on his prayers to Allah.

What happens on hajj?

There are a number of things that pilgrims must do to complete hajj.

These are:

1 putting on ihram
2 going round the Ka'bah seven times (tawaf)
3 a fast walk between As-Safa and Al-Marwah on the outskirts of Makkah
4 visiting Mina for midday prayers
5 standing at Arafat from noon to sunset
6 visiting Muzdalifah to collect pebbles
7 stoning the pillars in Mina
8 celebrating Id-ul-Adha.

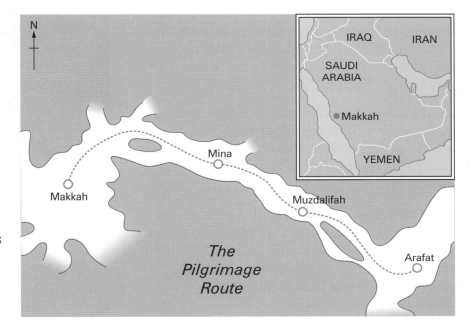

The Pilgrimage Route

During hajj, pilgrims are forbidden to:

• have sexual relations
• shave their hair or cut their nails
• use perfume or scented oils
• kill or hunt anything
• fight or argue
• (women) cover their faces, even if they would do so in their home country
• (men) wear clothes with stitching.

Activities

3 Look at the list alongside and with a partner discuss why these things are forbidden during hajj.

3.8 The meaning and significance of the events of hajj in Makkah (2)

The meaning of events in Makkah

Makkah is a place that is holy to all Muslims. It is so holy that no non-Muslim is allowed to enter. It was here that the Prophet Muhammad was not only born, but received the first message of God.

In the Great Mosque at Makkah is the Ka'bah. This is a simple cube-shaped building, 15 metres high. It is revered as the House of God, and Muslims believe it was built, on the order of Allah, by Ibrahim and Ismail. In one corner of the Ka'bah is the famous Black Stone, protected by a huge silver frame.

The Ka'bah is, quite literally, the focus of Islam, as it is toward the Ka'bah that all Muslims must face each time they pray, wherever they are in the world. Most mosques have a **qiblah** wall so that Muslims know which direction to face when praying.

The Ka'bah is draped with a black silk covering, the kiswa, beautifully embroidered with Qur'anic texts in gold and silver. This is replaced every year in a special ceremony that takes place one month before hajj.

Upon arriving in Makkah, pilgrims perform the initial **tawaf**, which is a circular, counter-clockwise procession around the Ka'bah. All the while, they are reciting 'Labbayka Allahumma Labbayk', which means, 'Here I am at your service, O God, Here I am!'

This action was commanded by Allah in the Qur'an:

> '… "Associate not anything (in worship) with Me; and sanctify My House for those who compass it round, or stand up, or bow, or prostrate themselves (therein in prayer)."' (Surah 22:26)

> 'And proclaim the Pilgrimage among men… Then let them complete the rites prescribed for them, perform their vows, and (again) circumambulate the Ancient House. Such (is the Pilgrimage): whoever honors the sacred rites of Allah, for him it is good in the sight of his Lord…' (Surah 22:27–30)

edexcel ::: key terms

qiblah – The direction of the Ka'bah in Makkah.

tawaf – Going round the Ka'bah seven times in worship of Allah.

Muslims performing tawaf at the start of hajj.

The tawaf is meant to awaken in each Muslim a consciousness that Allah is the centre of and the source of all meaning in their life. Each person gains their true identity from being part of the community of Muslim believers, known as the ummah. Circling the Ka'bah all together, wearing identical clothing, is an unforgettable experience that unites the pilgrims and shows that everyone is equal in the eyes of Allah.

For discussion

Hajj is a very special religious occasion. Discuss the significance of women not covering their faces when taking part in hajj.

The significance for Muslims in the events of hajj in Makkah

the Ka'bah is the earthly focus for prayer

reminds Muslims that they are part of the ummah

Why events in Makkah are significant

following in the footsteps of Muhammad

obeying Allah is the central focus of a Muslim's life

Makkah is the holiest city for Muslims

Hajj is designed to develop a deeper awareness of Allah and a sense of spiritual fulfilment. It is also believed to be an opportunity to seek forgiveness of sins accumulated throughout life. The Prophet Muhammad said that a person who performs hajj properly will be like a newborn baby, that is, free of all sins.

Visiting Makkah and performing hajj is both a duty and a privilege for a Muslim. The Ka'bah has unique significance as the first house of worship to be built for Allah and at any time of the day or night there will be Muslims around the world facing towards it and saying salah. The experience of circling this building with thousands of other Muslims is in itself a unique and moving experience, making the pilgrim realise how insignificant he is in comparison to Allah the Creator.

Activities

1 If possible watch a short video clip about hajj or talk to someone who has been to Makkah. Try to imagine what it must be like to be part of such a large group of people, all praising Allah. Now write a paragraph about why you think so many people every year are happy to sacrifice their time and their comfort to go on hajj.

Explain why the events at Makkah are important for Muslims during hajj. (8 marks)

■ **Basic, 1–2-mark answers**

Basic answers usually describe what happens in Makkah during hajj rather than giving reasons why these events are important for Muslims.

● **Good, 3–6-mark answers**

Level two answers (3–4 marks) tend to give just one or two simple reasons. Level three answers (5–6 marks) give more reasons or provide more developed reasons.

▲ **Excellent, 7–8-mark answers**

Most excellent answers will give four reasons why events at Makkah are important for Muslims during hajj. Other excellent answers will give fewer reasons but develop them. It is possible to get full marks by giving just one reason, but this would need to be explained in real depth.

Summary

Hajj is the fifth pillar of Islam and is the pilgrimage to Makkah. All adult Muslims should go to on hajj at least once in their lifetime if they are physically able to do so.

3.9 The meaning and significance of the events of hajj at Arafat

Learning outcomes

By the end of this lesson, you should be able to:

● state what happens at Arafat

● understand the significance of going to Arafat for a Muslim

● give an opinion, with reasons, about how standing at Arafat makes a difference to a Muslim.

edexcel ::: key terms

Arafat – A plain near Makkah where pilgrims confess their sins.

What happens at Arafat?

After the dawn prayer at Mina, pilgrims travel the 7 kilometres to the plain of **Arafat** where they spend the entire day in prayer. This is the climax of hajj.

Muslims believe that it was on the Mount of Mercy in Arafat that Adam and Eve, separated for 200 years following their expulsion from the Garden of Eden, recognised each other, were reunited and were forgiven by Allah for disobeying Him.

It is also believed that the Prophet Muhammad gave a famous sermon here.

Arafat is a huge plain without any shelter from the sun. During hajj over two million people converge on Arafat – on the foothills of the Mount of Mercy – stand bare headed and pray to Allah for forgiveness.

They are allowed parasols to protect them from the sun, but many prefer to suffer the heat as a sign that they remember the heat of the Day of Judgement and rely on Allah's mercy.

The pilgrim will recite the talbiyah (the words of Ibrahim) many times during the course of the day. It is said that when Allah forgives a sin for one servant at the place-of-standing (the plain of Arafat), Allah forgives it for everyone there who is guilty of it.

The importance of standing at Arafat and praying for forgiveness before Allah is emphasised by the Prophet Muhammad who said that anyone who had been present at Arafat would have performed hajj. This signified that even if the pilgrim arrived too late to start their pilgrimage at the Ka'bah, as long as they had taken part in the standing at Arafat their hajj would be accepted by Allah.

Pilgrims at Arafat during hajj.

In the newspaper the *Arab News* (19 December 2007) it was reported:

> Despite the hardships, pilgrims told how reaching the Arafat was a dream come true… For Jehangir Asmat, a Pakistani national, the standing at Arafat was a renewal of his faith. 'I feel like I've been born again and I've taken a vow to put my past behind me and start afresh and live life according to the strict tenets of Islam,' he said.

After going on hajj the pilgrim is entitled to be known as hajji. However, many Muslim scholars believe that this is only justified if hajj has changed the pilgrim's outlook and behaviour and was not just a series of rituals.

The standing at Arafat is both physically hard and emotionally intense. This signifies that a Muslim is prepared to abandon material possessions and physical comforts in order to achieve closeness to Allah and seek his forgiveness.

For discussion

It is impossible to describe the feeling of someone who has experienced the standing at Arafat. Can you describe any other experience that might make a person change their attitudes to their life?

The significance of standing at Arafat

- Allah forgives the sins Muslims confess so that they can start their lives afresh.
- Muslims show commitment to Allah by obeying His command and praying all day in the heat of the sun.
- Standing at Arafat is preparation for standing before Allah on the Day of Judgement.
- Taking part in this experience reminds Muslims that they are a small part of Allah's Creation and are dependent on Allah for their well-being. This develops humility.
- After this experience most Muslims (now hajjis) return home feeling better able to live their lives as Allah has commanded.

Activities

1 List as many reasons as you can think of why the events of hajj at Arafat are important for Muslims.
2 Which do you think is the most important reason? Explain why.

Summary

Arafat is where hajj pilgrims stand and pray to Allah for forgiveness for a whole day. It is the most important part of hajj.

3.10 The meaning and significance of the events of hajj at Mina

80

Hajj pilgrims, stoning the pillars at Mina.

When the pilgrims leave Arafat they go to Muzdalifah, a valley that is half way between Arafat and Mina, where they spend the night. They pick up small stones, or pebbles, for the duty of stoning, which they do over the next few days in Mina. The stones should be small, the size of large peas. As they will be stoning the jamaraat or pillars seven or ten times, with seven pebbles each time, they need to pick up 49 or 70 pebbles. If they do not pick these up in Muzdalifah, they can pick them up in Mina.

When they arrive at Mina on the tenth day, the pebbles are thrown. Following the Prophet's example, the pebbles should not be thrown before sunrise on this day.

What is the meaning of the stoning?

At Mina there are three large pillars that represent Satan and which Muslims believe stand at the places where Ibrahim was tempted by the devil to disobey Allah and refuse to sacrifice his son Ismail.

Sometimes taking part in an action can help you to understand a belief. The pilgrims have been forgiven by Allah at Arafat and are now showing their belief that Satan is always around to tempt them to do wrong.

Taking part in stoning the pillars helps Muslims understand that Satan needs to be stopped from having an effect on their lives. As they throw the stones they are remembering their bad traits and showing the intention to improve themselves.

The pilgrims camp at Mina for two or three days. They stone the pillars again, but the main focus is to remember how Ibrahim resisted Satan and obeyed Allah, being prepared to give everything, even his son, to show his love for God. They remember how Allah provided an animal for Ibrahim to sacrifice, and they sacrifice an animal in the same way. The pilgrims eat some of the meat and any excess is frozen by the Saudi Arabian government and eventually given to the poor. This is the celebration of Id-ul-Adha (see pages 82–83). They also shave the hair from their heads (women cut off at least 2 cm) and many return to their normal clothes.

Why is Mina significant?

At Mina, by taking part in a simple yet pictorial action, the pilgrims are reinforcing the promises they made at Arafat when, having had their sins forgiven, they committed themselves to live a better life and follow the commands of Allah more carefully. Most of the time at Mina is spent reading the Qur'an, listening to talks and joining in discussions about various aspects of Islam in preparation for returning home. On the third day, the pilgrims return to Makkah and hajj is complete.

Hajj contains the same lessons as salah, zakah and sawm and is an example of total submission to Allah.

Activities

1 Imagine you are a pilgrim at Mina. Send a message home to your family describing how you felt when you stoned the pillars.

Activities

2 Complete the chart explaining how different actions on hajj show equality that you began in Activity 1 in Section 3.8 (1) (page 74).

3 Go back over your lessons on salah, zakah, sawm and hajj. Find at least three common things that they teach about Islam.

Summary

Going to Mina and stoning the pillars symbolises the pilgrims rejecting Satan and preparing to return home spiritually refreshed.

3.11 The meaning and significance of the celebration of Id-ul-Adha

Learning outcomes

By the end of this lesson, you should be able to:

● describe what happens on Id-ul-Adha

● explain why this festival is significant to all Muslims

● evaluate, with reasons, why this festival is a significant part of hajj.

edexcel ⣿ key terms

Id-ul-Adha – The festival of the sacrifice.

For discussion

What would you be prepared to do for someone you loved? Would you give up a kidney to save a sibling's life?

Have you ever had to give up something that is very important to you? It is often said that we do not really appreciate something until we lose it.

In the story of Ibrahim and his son Ismail, Muslims have an example of someone who loved Allah so much that he was prepared to give up everything – even to sacrifice his son – to show his love and obedience to Allah.

Activities

1 Find out about the story of Ibrahim and his son Ismail. How is it remembered at both the beginning and end of hajj?

The festival of **Id-ul-Adha** is a time when Muslims all over the world remember how strong Ibrahim's faith in Allah was. Every Muslim takes part in the feast, not just those on hajj. It is a family occasion for the whole family of Islam, not just individual families. Preparations take place well in advance and on the actual day shops and schools are closed in Muslim countries so that everyone can take part.

Men who have completed hajj shave their heads after the animal has been sacrificed.

The animal to be sacrificed must be killed in a halal way by a specially trained person (see pages 90–91) and in the UK this has to be done in an abattoir. The meat is divided up for the poor, for friends and for relatives.

After the sacrifice for those at hajj, men will shave their heads and women will cut off at least 2 cm of their hair, and they will all remove their ihram and return to their normal clothing.

When everything is ready prayers will be said at the mosque and then the family will eat the meat.

The feast is celebrated by Muslims everywhere and is a way that those who did not go on hajj can join in the final activity. It is a reminder that their religion is not new but was ordained by Allah from the beginning. It reinforces the Muslim ummah and is very important as a sign of the power of Allah to unite different races into a common brotherhood.

Hajj is the most difficult of the pillars in many ways, as it involves great expense, travelling, giving up comfort, being away from home and spending many hours in hot sun, which is physically exhausting. The final sacrifice of an animal is not only in remembrance of Ibrahim but also is symbolic of the sacrifice made for Allah to show obedience and a reminder that all Muslims are members of one community striving to please their God.

Muslims celebrating the feast of Id-ul-Adha.

What is the significance of Id-ul-Adha?

This festival is important because:

- it reminds Muslims that Allah is great and that they must try to worship Allah in every aspect of their lives
- it helps those who were not on hajj to share the spirit of hajj with those of their family or community who were able to go to Makkah and reinforces the feeling of the ummah
- the sacrifice of an animal reminds Muslims that they should be prepared to give up everything to serve Allah
- the history behind the various activities of hajj reminds Muslims that their faith is not new but was, they believe, ordained by Allah from the very beginning of time.

Hajj is the fifth pillar of Islam and incorporates all aspects of the other pillars. All the pillars remind Muslims of Allah and help them to draw closer to Allah.

Activities

2   Create a wall display with the five pillars as headings. Under each heading write down how the pillar helps a Muslim to become closer to Allah. Some things will be the same for all of the pillars, for example 'shows obedience'.

Results Plus
Build Better Answers

'Celebrating festivals is a waste of time.'
In your answer you should refer to Islam.
(i) Do you agree? Give reasons for your answer. (3 marks)
(ii) Give reasons why some people might disagree with you. (3 marks)

■   **Basic, 1-mark answers**

These answers will give one basic reason. Be aware of the difference between saying what you think and giving reasons why you think it.

●   **Good, 2-mark answers**

These will either give two brief reasons or one developed reason. 'Developed' means you say something extra to explain your reason.

▲   **Excellent, 3-mark answers**

Answers that get full marks will either give three brief reasons or two developed reasons. They could also give one reason, but this would need to be fully developed.

Summary

Id-ul-Adha is the festival of sacrifice that takes place at the end of hajj. It reminds Muslims that nothing is too valuable to be given up for Allah.

examzone

Introduction

This section is all about why Muslims follow the Five Pillars of Islam. The examination paper will not ask you to describe or outline any of the pillars, but you need to know what Muslims do in order to understand and evaluate the significance of each one.

Quick quiz

1 Name the first pillar of Islam.
2 What happens during Id-ul-Fitr?
3 What should Muslims do before salah?
4 What is 'zakah'?
5 What should Muslims refrain from during Ramadan?
6 Give four reasons why Muslims fast during Ramadan.
7 Who should go on hajj?
8 What happens at Makkah during hajj?
9 What happens at Arafat during hajj?
10 What happens at Mina during hajj?

Find out more

Go to www.pearsonhotlinks.co.uk (express code 4264P) and click on the link for 'BBC Religion website' for more information about the Five Pillars.

Plenary activity

- Salah is every day.
- Sawm is one lunar month per year.
- Zakah is one payment per year.
- Hajj is once in a lifetime.

Discuss with a friend which pillar you think is the most difficult for a Muslim to keep and give three reasons for your point of view.

Self-evaluation checklist

How well have you understood the topics in this section? In the first column of the table below use the following code to rate your understanding:

Green – I understand this fully.

Orange – I am confident I can answer most questions on this.

Red – I need to do a lot more work on this topic.

In the second and third columns you need to think about:

- ● whether you have an opinion on this topic and could give reasons for that opinion, if asked.
- ● whether you can give the opinion of someone who disagrees with you and give reasons for this alternative opinion.

Content covered	My understanding is red/orange/ green	Can I give my opinion?	Can I give an alternative opinion?
● The meaning of the Shahadah			
● The significance of the Shahadah			
● What is involved in the practice of salah			
● Why salah is significant			
● What is involved in the practice of zakah			
● Why zakah is significant			
● The relationship of zakah to the ummah			
● What is involved in the practice of sawm during Ramadan			
● Why sawm is significant			
● The reasons and benefits of fasting			
● The meaning of Id-ul-Fitr			
● The significance of Id-ul-Fitr			
● The meaning of the events of hajj in Makkah			
● The significance of the events of hajj in Makkah			
● The meaning of the events of hajj at Arafat			
● The significance of the events of hajj at Arafat			
● The meaning of the events of hajj at Mina			
● The significance of the events of hajj at Mina			
● The meaning of the celebration of Id-ul-Adha			
● The significance of the celebration of Id-ul-Adha			

Introduction

In the exam you will see a choice of two questions on this module. Each question will include four tasks, which test your knowledge, understanding and evaluation of the material covered. A 2-mark question will ask you to define a term; a 4-mark question will ask your opinion on a point of view; an 8-mark question will ask you to explain a particular belief or idea; a 6-mark question will ask for your opinion on a point of view and ask you to consider an alternative point of view.

You must give your opinion, but must also include the reasons for your opinion. You need to give two reasons – any more than this and you will be wasting valuable time. For example, (1) I think that fasting makes someone a better Muslim because it is a pillar of Islam and therefore they are obeying the command of Allah. (2) Fasting encourages self-discipline by reminding them of the poor.

This question is always split into two parts and you should answer each part separately. For at least one of the parts you must refer to Muslim beliefs, and it's probably a good idea to consider what Muslims think first and then either use that for your own opinion or for the alternative opinion in (ii).

Mini exam paper

(a) What is **wudu**? (2 marks)

(b) Do you think fasting makes someone a better Muslim?

Give **two** reasons for your point of view. (4 marks)

(c) Explain why prayer (salah) is important for Muslims. (8 marks)

(d) 'The visit to Arafat is the most important part of hajj.'

In your answer you should refer to Islam.

(i) Do you agree? Give reasons for your opinion. (3 marks)

(ii) Give reasons why some people may disagree with you. (3 marks)

Give a glossary definition. You do not need to write any more – often this can be done in one sentence.

This question is worth the most so it is important that you spend some time on it. 'Explain why' means that you need to give reasons. A good answer here will often give four reasons, but you could give fewer reasons and still produce a good response if you develop them. This is also the question where you should double-check the quality of your spelling and punctuation. Remember to take care when writing your answers, and to use proper sentences and not bullet points.

Mark scheme

(a) You will earn **2 marks** for a correct answer, and **1 mark** for a partially correct answer.

(b) To earn up to the full **4 marks** you need to give two reasons (as asked) and develop them. Two brief reasons or one developed reason will earn **2 marks** and one reason without development will earn **1 mark**.

(c) You can earn **7–8 marks** by giving up to four reasons, but the fewer reasons you give, the more you must develop them. You are being assessed on your use of language, so you also need to take care to express your understanding in a clear style of English and make some use of specialist vocabulary.

(d) To go beyond **3 marks** for the whole of this question you must refer to Islam. The more you are able to develop your reasons the more marks you will earn. Three simple reasons can earn you the same mark as one developed reason.

ResultsPlus
Build Better Answers

(d) 'The visit to Arafat is the most important part of hajj.'
In your answer you should refer to Islam.
(i) Do you agree? Give reasons for your opinion. (3 marks)
(ii) Give reasons why some people may disagree with you. (3 marks)

Student answer	Comments	Improved student answer
(i) I think going to Arafat is the most important part of hajj because people have to stand all day in the sun and give up their comfort for Allah. It is at Arafat that people confess their sins.	This candidate clearly knows what happens at Arafat but has not quite understood the importance of this event for Muslims. Both parts of the answer give two brief reasons and this makes it a good answer, with some room for improvement.	(i) Arafat is the most important part of hajj because it is at Arafat that people confess their sins. Allah forgives them and they can go away and start their lives afresh. It is also a sign of commitment to Allah because they stand all day in the hot sun praying to Allah in preparation for the Day of Judgement.
(ii) Some people disagree with me because all of hajj is very difficult and expensive. Also, visiting the Ka'bah and going round it is very special.		(ii) However, some people would disagree with me because all parts of hajj are part of the overall experience in obedience to Allah. Going to visit the Ka'bah in Makkah and stoning the pillars at Mina also have great meaning for Muslims. Finally, going on hajj itself is very expensive both in time and money and is a sign of commitment to the will of Allah.

Living the Muslim life

Introduction

In this section you will learn about the way Muslims live in order to please Allah. You will also learn about and reflect on the problems that could arise for Muslims living in a mainly non-Muslim society.

'Islam' is an Arabic word that means 'submission' or 'obedience' and to be a Muslim one must be ready to obey all the commands given by Allah. This obedience is a positive act that brings all one's wishes and everything one does in line with the will of Allah and so gives peace of mind and happiness in all areas of one's life. In Section 1 you learned about the belief of tawhid and how it affects the life of a Muslim. In this section you will learn and evaluate the practical effects this belief has on the way Muslims live their daily lives.

Learning outcomes for this section

By the end of this section you should be able to:

- give definitions of the key terms and use them in answer to GCSE questions
- know the meaning and significance of halal and haram
- understand the teaching about greater and lesser jihad and its effects on a Muslim's life
- evaluate the implications of living a Muslim life in a non-Muslim society
- express your point of view, with reasons, about the issues raised for Muslims living in a non-Muslim society
- explain the efforts of a Muslim organisation working to relieve poverty and suffering in the UK and the reasons why this charity does this work.

edexcel ⠿ key terms

aqiqa	haram	madrasah
capitalism	hijab	riba
Dar-ul-Islam	janazah prayers	sadaqah
greater jihad		
halal	lesser jihad	

Fascinating fact

More than 1.6 million Muslims live in the UK, and roughly half of them live in London.

Muslim teacher must not wear niqab in class

Christian air hostess not to wear cross when in uniform

Primary school refuses to provide halal food, parents complain

Fatwa causes anger by allowing blind Muslim to bring dog into mosque

Sikhs told wearing turbans dangerous in factories

French president thinks Muslim veils debase women

1 Look up the meanings of the key terms. Make two columns and divide the terms into those actions that might affect a Muslim's life everyday and those that are more long-term actions.

2 The UK is a multi-faith society. It is also multicultural. This can be a good thing but it can also cause problems. Sometimes the media print stories that are designed to shock people and give the wrong impression of the different religions and traditions in society today. The headlines shown on this page were in the news in 2008. Find out more about the stories behind them, or other stories like this. Do you think they were fairly reported? Give reasons for your point of view.

4.1 The meaning and significance of the concepts of halal and haram

Learning outcomes

By the end of this lesson, you should be able to:

- explain the meaning of halal and haram
- explain why obeying these commands is important for Muslims
- evaluate, with reasons, the effect of these rules on the life of a Muslim.

edexcel key terms

Dar-ul-Islam – The abode of Islam/lands ruled by the Shari'ah.

halal – That which is permitted or lawful.

haram – That which is forbidden or unlawful.

How do Muslims make decisions about how to live – halal and haram?

As we grow up we learn that there are some things that we can do that please people, parents, friends, etc. and some things that make people cross.

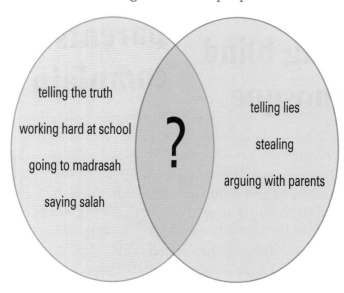

At home and at school there are certain rules that you have to obey in order to keep the family or school running smoothly. These rules might be simple and easy to keep, like making your bed every day, or more difficult, like not talking in class. Keeping to the rules helps everyone in the community work together and feel secure.

Muslims also have rules that are part of their religion and help them live lives that please Allah. These rules are commanded by Allah in the Holy Qur'an and fall into two main groups, **halal**, things that are allowed, and **haram**, things that are forbidden.

For Muslims, Islam is not just a system of beliefs but a complete way of life, and knowing what is halal and what is haram is important so that they can please Allah in all aspects of life.

Actions and things that are forbidden, haram, are clearly written in the Qur'an. There is no doubt about them, and Muslims believe doing these things brings punishment from Allah and bars their entry into Paradise.

Everything else that is not haram is halal, but there are some things that, although they are not forbidden, are not considered the best things to do. So in all there are five groups into which actions fall:

- haram – forbidden, for example sex outside marriage
- makruh – discouraged, for example divorce
- mubah – neutral
- mustahab – recommended, for example du'a prayer
- fard or wajib – obligatory, for example observing the Five Pillars.

How does observing halal and haram affect the life of a Muslim?

Activities

1   Look at the list below. Think of a week in your life. Now make a chart of the things you would not have been able to do if you were a Muslim.

Examples of haram:

- Setting anyone equal with Allah

- Being unkind to parents

- Being unfair in business

- Charging interest on a loan

- Pre-marital sex

- Certain foods

- Alcohol

The full list of things that are haram can be found in Surahs 4 and 6.

The significance of halal and haram

The concepts of halal and haram are significant to Muslims because:

- they are commanded by Allah in the Qur'an and Muslims believe that obeying Allah enables them to lead a good life and brings rewards in the next life
- they were followed and taught by the Prophet Muhammad and all Muslims should follow his example
- observing halal and haram clearly identifies one as a Muslim and strengthens the fellowship between Muslims
- observing halal and haram constantly reminds a Muslim of the teachings of Allah and that Islam is a way of life.

Many Muslims find it difficult to balance their everyday lives in a non-Muslim country with the commands of Allah. Countries where Shari'ah law is kept are called **Dar-ul-Islam**.

Activities

2   Do you think it would be easier to keep halal in Dar-ul-Islam countries?

3   One Muslim said that 'although we are surrounded by what seems to be haram everywhere we look, it is the presence of such things which often allows us to positively reinforce the teachings of Islam in our daily lives'. How far do you think this statement is true? Write a short paragraph explaining your point of view.

ResultsPlus
Watch out!

Many students only focus on food laws when they answer questions on the principles of haram and halal – remember that certain foods are just one of many things that are haram!

Summary

All Muslims try to live their lives in obedience to Allah's commands. This means being very careful to observe the rules regarding actions that are haram.

4.2 Islamic teaching on greater and lesser jihad and the effects of this teaching on a Muslim's life

Learning outcomes

By the end of this lesson, you should be able to:

● describe and explain the teaching on lesser and greater jihad

● show you understand the effects of this teaching on the life of a Muslim

● evaluate, with reasons, the significance of this teaching for Muslims.

edexcel ⠿ key terms

greater jihad – Struggle to overcome evil in one's own life.

lesser jihad – Struggle in the cause of Islam to overcome injustice in society.

Every day we make choices about what to do, where to go, who to see. These are all small things that might not make much difference to the world in general but do make a difference to how we see ourselves. We have to choose the best thing to do, which is not always easy and is often very difficult.

Muslims believe that in order to obey Allah they must always be thinking about the right way to live. This struggle to do right, which takes place in our minds, is called **greater jihad**. Jihad means 'to strive'. The thought bubbles show some of the everyday decisions Muslims have to make that are part of greater jihad.

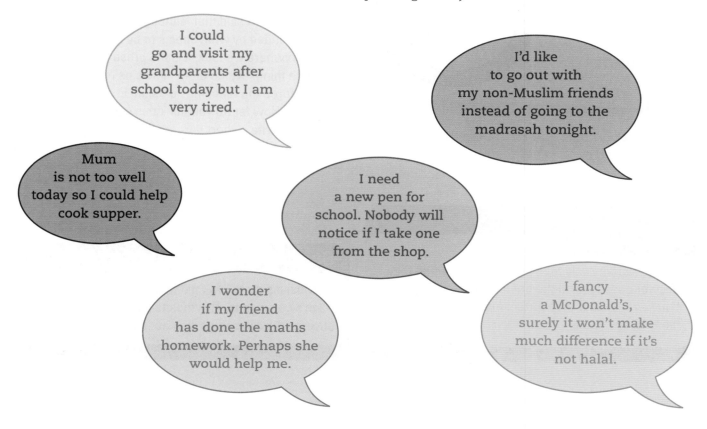

For discussion

'Not always doing the right thing only affects the individual so it's not worth worrying about.'

How far do you agree with this statement? Give reasons for your point of view.

For discussion

In class discuss a recent report you have seen or read about a war and decide if it is accurately describing lesser jihad. Give at least two reasons for your decision.

For a Muslim, the struggle – greater jihad – is to do the will of Allah, avoid anything that is haram and evil and get closer to Allah. This means reading the Qur'an, following the Five Pillars and observing Shari'ah.

Activities

1   Write a short story that would help a very young Muslim understand about the greater jihad.

The word jihad is also referred to as 'holy war'. Greater jihad is the 'war within us' but there is also what is often called **lesser jihad.** This is actually striving to preserve the supremacy of Allah and protect the faith of Islam. Newspaper stories and television news programmes often mistakenly refer to any war in a Muslim country or any act of violence by Muslims as jihad.

There are set rules for lesser jihad.

Why war?

Rules for:	Rules against:
in defence against an attacker	to gain land
to protect the oppressed	indiscriminate use of violence, such as killing civilians
to preserve the Islamic way of life	to start the fight
declared by a recognised and respected religious leader	must not be declared for political reasons

Activities

2   Look at the picture above and reflect on whether the damage done would be acceptable as jihad.

3   Write a letter to a friend explaining why a personal struggle is called 'greater jihad' and a military struggle is called 'lesser jihad'.

Watch out!

Read the question carefully. Some candidates see the word 'jihad' and just write about 'holy war'. The question might be looking for an answer on greater jihad so check it again before you start writing.

Summary

- Jihad means 'to struggle'.
- Lesser jihad refers to fighting for the cause of Islam and has very strict guidelines.
- Greater jihad is the struggle each Muslim has to lead a life that is pleasing to Allah.

4.3 The meaning and significance of Islamic birth rituals

Learning outcomes

By the end of this lesson, you should be able to:

● describe Islamic birth rites

● explain why they take place

● evaluate, with reasons, the significance of the rites to a Muslim.

edexcel ⠿ key terms

aqiqa – The birth ceremony for Muslim children.

madrasah – Qur'anic school attached to the mosque.

What happens when a baby is born?

Action	Meaning
The adhan (Allah is great) is whispered into the right ear, and the iqamah (come to prayer) is also recited into the left ear, by the head of the family or the most senior male present.	The first words the baby should hear are Allah Akbar – Allah is great. This sets the scene for the rest of their life.
Aqiqa – this takes place seven days after birth. There is a family celebration when the baby is named (see below). Also, the head is shaved and traditionally a sum of money is given to the poor equal in value to the weight of the hair.	The celebrations welcome the baby to the family of Islam, shaving the head follows the sunnah of the Prophet and the giving of money means that the joy is shared with the poor.
Naming – this is part of the aqiqa ceremony. It should be a name with a religious meaning and is chosen by the parents.	Acknowledging that the child is a member of the ummah.
Khitan – circumcision of boys, following the command of Allah.	Obeying the commands of Allah and showing submission to Allah.
At about four years old the child begins its formal Islamic education and will start to go to the **madrasah**.	Learning how to become a full and serving member of the ummah.

Activities

1 Imagine you were visiting a Muslim family when a new baby had been born. Write a diary of the celebrations you saw.

Whispering into the baby's ear.

What is the significance of these ceremonies to a Muslim?

Babies are welcomed into families across the world.

1 For Muslims there is extra joy as they are obeying the will of Allah to have children and increase the ummah.

2 Everything that takes place in the first week (if possible) of a baby's life follows the sunnah of the Prophet so is very significant.

3 The ceremonies draw attention to the belief that the baby should have the opportunity to grow up as a Muslim, which is very important to Muslims.

4 The ceremonies centre the attention of the family and the community on their responsibilities to help the baby become a good Muslim. This is continued as the child grows up and is taught about Islam, firstly at home, and then formally, when the child begins to attend madrasah and mosque. This is commanded by Allah.

Some people might think that it is not fair to assume that the baby will want to be a Muslim, and therefore they believe these birth rites are unnecessary and that the child should be able to choose when it is older.

Activities

2 How far do you think it is important to carry out these ceremonies? Write a short paragraph explaining your views. Give reasons for your point of view.

Everyone is born a Muslim. It is the upbringing of a child that decides if the person continues to be a Muslim or to follow another faith.

For discussion

Look at the statement above. What do you think it means? Do you think it makes a difference to the upbringing of a child?

Summary

Birth ceremonies are important to Muslims because they are following the will of Allah and the sunnah of the Prophet. They are the beginning of the child's upbringing in the Muslim faith and remind the family and the community of their responsibility towards the baby.

4.4 The meaning and significance of Islamic death rituals

Learning outcomes

By the end of this lesson, you should be able to:

- describe Islamic death rites
- explain the meaning of the rites
- evaluate, with reasons, the significance of these rites to a Muslim.

edexcel key terms

janazah prayers – The special salah used at funerals.

What happens when someone dies?

'...to Allah we belong, and to Him is our return.' (Surah 2:156)

There is always sadness when someone's life ends. Family and friends know they are going to miss the person who has died.

The belief that there is a life after death for people who have obeyed Allah gives comfort to Muslims as they know that their loved one has gone to a better place. Death is just a gateway to another, eternal life.

The various rites that take place after death are all connected to the belief that this life is a preparation for the next life.

1 Ghusl – the washing of the body. Symbolically this removes the impurity caused by sin. Before burial, when a Muslim is being prepared to face Allah on Judgement Day, the impurities caused by sin must be removed. Only martyrs are exempt from this as the act of martyrdom removes sin.

2 The body is anointed with camphor and wrapped in clean white cloth. This is part of the belief that a body must be as clean and pleasant as possible. Many people who have completed hajj are buried in their ihram.

3 Prayers – salat-ul-**janazah**. The community gathers, and the imam (prayer leader) stands in front of the body, facing qiblah. The body is placed with its head facing to the right, and its feet to the left, of the prayer leader. The funeral prayer is said standing, with no bowing or prostration. The iman recites specific prayers which the mourners repeat alongside.

4 A simple funeral is held. After the prayers, only the men go to the graveside. If possible the body should be carried and no money wasted on expensive funeral cars. In countries where it is allowed, the body will be buried without a coffin. Muslims do not agree with cremation. Mourners will walk to the cemetery. The body will be buried resting on its right side, facing Makkah-quiblah.

All this is meant to remind Muslims that Allah determines who will live and who will die. Death is simply returning to Allah and money should not be spent glorifying the dead – rather mourners should remember Allah and Allah's greatness.

5 Relatives observe a three-day mourning period. Mourners avoid wearing jewellery or decorative clothes and will be prepared to receive visitors who wish to share their grief. Widows spend a period of four months and ten days in mourning called iddah, in accordance with the teaching of the Qur'an.

For Muslims, everything they do in life is preparation for akhirah, life after death. Life is a test and how one deals with the test determines what will happen after death. Death is just another step towards akhirah. Allah created humans and has promised that one day they will return to Him and be judged on their lives.

'From the (earth) did We create you, and into it shall We return you, and from it shall We bring you out once again.' (Surah 20:55)

What is the significance of these rituals to a Muslim?

As in life so in death everything must put Allah at the forefront of a Muslim's thinking and actions.

Muslims believe that death is part of life and the beginning of the life after death. As such it should be handled with as much respect as possible for the deceased person without detracting from the greatness of Allah. Ceremonies are simple and carried out as quickly as possible so that the dead person can start their new life as soon as possible.

Everything, including money, is given by Allah and should not be wasted on unnecessary things in life or expensive funerals after death, which in itself is only a gateway to a better world. Time should be spent praising Allah for His goodness and praying for the well-being of the dead person.

Activities

1 How far do you think that the ceremonies connected with death in Islam reflect the belief in a life after death? Write a short paragraph giving your point of view with at least two reasons.

For discussion

'Money spent on funerals shows how much you care for the person.'

Organise a debate on this topic with some speakers supporting the statement and some speakers against the statement. Make a note of the arguments used by both sides. Include an Islamic viewpoint.

Summary

Muslim funerals are simple and reflect the Muslim belief that Allah is great and death is the beginning of life after death.

4.5 The meaning and importance of Muslim attitudes to drugs and alcohol

Learning outcomes

By the end of this lesson, you should be able to:

- explain Muslim attitudes to drugs and alcohol
- show how this attitude affects a Muslim's way of life
- evaluate, with reasons, the importance of obeying these laws in the life of a Muslim.

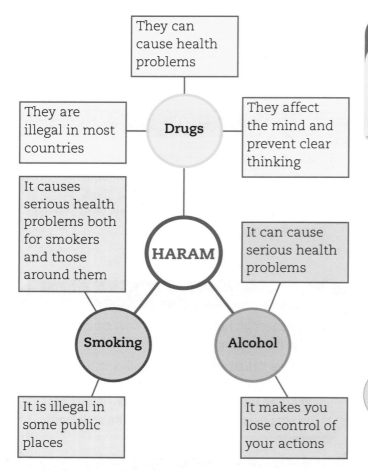

Activities

1 Look at the diagram on the left and the hadith below it. How do the two link together? Draw a new diagram linking the two with an explanation of how you have created the links.

Why do Muslims keep these laws?

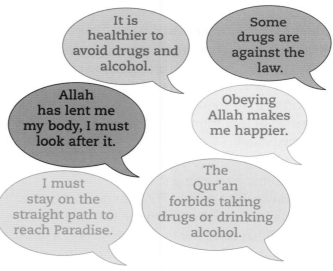

It is healthier to avoid drugs and alcohol.

Some drugs are against the law.

Allah has lent me my body, I must look after it.

Obeying Allah makes me happier.

I must stay on the straight path to reach Paradise.

The Qur'an forbids taking drugs or drinking alcohol.

There is a hadith that says that on the Day of Judgement everyone will be asked four things concerning:

- their body and how they used it
- their life and how they spent it
- their wealth and how they earned it
- their knowledge and what they did with it.

Does it matter if these Islamic laws are ignored?

Islam is not just a religious belief, it is a complete way of life. To be a Muslim means to follow the Shari'ah or 'straight path'. This is a clear code of conduct based on the Qur'an, and the sunnah and hadith of the Prophet. Not to obey the laws of Allah means that you are not a Muslim.

Muslims believe that life is a test and everything that happens, every problem they face and every good thing they enjoy, has come from Allah. How they deal with situations, whether good or bad, decides what will happen to them after death. Those who pass the test by obeying Allah will be rewarded and those who fail will be punished.

Muslims believe that alcohol makes people lose control and behave in ways that they would not normally.

Recreational drugs and alcohol are haram in Islam, so Muslims believe those who ignore this rule will be punished in the life after death. However, there are other reasons why many Muslims would not use these:

- They can cause people to commit other sins, as people lose control of their actions.
- It is easy to become addicted to either drugs or alcohol and this leads to problems with work and relationships and in some cases totally ruins a life.
- They can cause serious damage to the body.

It also forbidden for Muslims to buy or sell alcohol or to work in any job that promotes alcohol, drugs or tobacco. This is to prevent them being the cause of someone else committing sin.

Not drinking alcohol or taking drugs could cause difficulties for Muslims who have to mix socially with non-Muslims. However, many non-Muslims recognise the dangers associated with these things and refuse to participate as well.

Activities

2   Imagine you are a Muslim going away from home to college. Make a list of the problems you might face with some suggestions of what you might need to do. Include some of the things you have already learned.

3   How important is it to follow the rules of Islam? Write a play that shows your answer to this question. Make sure you include a character with a viewpoint different from your own.

Results**Plus**
Build Better Answers

Do you think Muslim attitudes to drugs and alcohol are out of date?
Give **two** reasons for your point of view. (4 marks)

 Basic, 1-mark answers

Basic answers give their opinion and only back it up with a brief reason for this opinion.

 Good, 2–3-mark answers

A 2-mark answer will give an opinion supported by two brief reasons or one developed reason. A 3-mark answer will give one brief and one developed reason for the opinion.

 Excellent, 4-mark answers

Answers that receive full marks will give their opinion and support it with two developed reasons.

Summary

Drugs and alcohol are forbidden in Islam because they are injurious to health and can cause Muslims to lose sight of their main goal, which is to please Allah.

4.6 The implications of Muslim laws on dress when living in a western society

Learning outcomes

By the end of this lesson, you should be able to:

- describe the Muslim laws on dress
- explain the importance of these rules to Muslims
- evaluate the importance of observing these laws in a western society.

edexcel key terms

hijab – The headscarf worn by Muslim women.

The hijab or headscarf.

The burqa.

The key word with regard to Muslim dress laws is modesty (see Surah 24: 30–31). This is interpreted in different ways in different cultures, but basically no man or woman should dress in such a way that the shape of their body is obvious to others. These rules begin at the age of puberty, so in schools Muslim students have to be careful how they dress for PE lessons. Baggy tracksuits are fine.

Rules for women	Rules for men
modesty	modesty
cover whole body except face and hands	cover at least navel to knees
loose non-transparent clothing	loose non-transparent clothing
not dress like men	not dress like women
	not wear silk or gold

Although **hijab** is usually understood to be the headscarf that covers the hair, in many Muslim groups now it is interpreted more generally as modest dress, which includes the headscarf.

As you can see from the photographs, Muslim women interpret these rules in different ways. Some women choose to wear the burqa or the veil because they believe:

- it creates anonymity
- it gives security
- people judge them for who they are not what they look like.

Muslim women from primary school to university choose to wear Islamic modest dress. This does not prevent them from studying or participating fully in academic life. They go on to follow successful careers of their own choice in many different fields. Hijab does not prevent Muslim women from following their dreams. For example, numerous Muslim women participated successfully in the 2008 Olympic Games wearing the hijab/Islamic modest clothing.

At a college in Bolton many of the Muslim girls in the sixth form wear the veil. Their dress, they say, 'is about their faith and cultural identity, not about wanting to be separate'.

One girl who has been wearing the veil only since entering the sixth form, did so against the wishes of her parents, who feared it would be a barrier to her getting on at college. She says that has not been the case: 'I cannot see the difference between me wearing the veil and others who don't. A lot of my teachers are male, but we get on so well. They know my personality. I can express myself just like any other person. A lot of my friends communicate through chat lines. They don't see each other, but don't have any difficulty. What's the difference?'

Another, who is studying psychology, IT and history A-levels with a view to reading history at Manchester University, has been wearing the veil since Year 7. She is adamant that it does not impede communication and that girls cannot hide their feelings behind it. She joked that chewing gum was about the only thing she might get away with.

(From an article by Elaine Williams published in the *Times Educational Supplement* on 1 December 2006)

What are the implications of wearing Muslim dress in a western society

- Wearing the veil has become a political issue in some countries and has caused many people to question whether banning it is against a woman's basic human rights.
- Many feminists and others consider that the hijab is oppressive and unfair to women.
- Many Muslim women wear the hijab as an expression of their identity and commitment to Islam and not through a desire to be seen as different. Wearers can receive abuse in some situations and yet choose to wear the hijab despite this danger because they are sure of the reasons they are wearing it.
- Many Muslim women believe that by wearing the hijab they are interpreting the teaching of the Qur'an in the best possible way by fulfilling Allah's command to dress modestly.

Activities

1. Having read the article about the sixth form girls, discuss whether you think that the dress rules, especially for girls, are good or bad? Do they protect the girls or do they prevent them from having freedom? Then make a list of the difficulties Muslims teenagers might face in a British comprehensive school and suggest ways they might overcome them.

For discussion

- Many schools place restrictions on Muslim girls wearing any form of specific religious dress, such as the hijab, burqa or niqab. What do you think about this? Give reasons for your point of view.
- How far do you think it should be a person's choice as to how they dress in society?

Although covering the face is a matter of local tradition and choice in Islam, there has been great debate about the decision by the president of France to authorise a law that forbids any clear sign of religious affiliation in French state-run schools. This law, sometimes called the 'veil law', was voted in by the French parliament in March 2004. It forbids the wearing of any clearly religious articles, such as the Islamic hijab, the Jewish kippa or large Christian crosses (and thus affects both girls and boys). This is the same in some Muslim countries, such as Indonesia and Turkey, which also ban the hijab in their state-run schools.

Summary

Muslim dress is an expression of obedience to the will of Allah, who commands that both men and women should dress modestly. Various aspects of women's dress are a matter of individual choice or, in some cases, the law, culture and traditions of the country in which they live.

4.7 The implications of Muslim laws on food when living in a western society

102

> ### Learning outcomes
>
> By the end of this lesson, you should be able to:
> ● describe Muslim food laws
> ● explain why these laws exist
> ● evaluate the importance of these laws in the life of a Muslim.

Whether food is halal can be checked on the list of ingredients.

How often do you read the food information on the back of a food packet? Would you know what all the ingredients were? People who have food allergies or special religious diets have to be careful what food they eat. This means checking for certain ingredients even in the smallest things, like jelly beans.

Muslims have rules about what they can eat and what they can do. These are laid down in the Qur'an. In the Qur'an, Allah has told Muslims to eat halal food (food that is allowed), and not to eat haram food (food that is not allowed).

Halal	Haram
beef, lamb, chicken (but all meat must be killed in a special way)	pigs
fish with fins and scales	shellfish, e.g. mussels
fruits, vegetables, nuts	reptiles
milk, honey	all alcohol

Much of the food sold in stores these days contains something haram. For example, many sweets contain gelatin, which comes from pigs or other haram animals. Many cheeses contain rennet, an ingredient that is haram if it comes from an animal that is not prepared in the special way that Muslims believe Allah has commanded.

The Qur'an says: '*O ye people! Eat of what is on earth, lawful and good; and do not follow the footsteps of Satan...*' (Surah 2:168)

Muslims believe that Allah has given them regulations about food and drink in order to protect their health. Also, following the commands of Allah regarding food encourages self-discipline and constantly reminds Muslims that everything they do is part of ibadah (see pages 6–7).

This is also shown by Muslims beginning and ending their meals with praise to Allah for the good things Allah has given them.

Anything that is not specifically mentioned in the Qur'an as haram is allowed and should be enjoyed. Everything Muslims eat is included in these rules – it makes no difference whether they are at a state banquet or in a one-room flat.

Meat must be killed in a halal way. This involves cutting the throat of the animal with a very sharp knife, and Muslims will not eat meat that has been shot or electrocuted as they regard these methods as cruel. Many people do not agree with the methods used in halal butchers, but Muslims believe that the animal should be killed as quickly and painlessly as possible and not experience the terror of the slaughter house. (Many Muslims also disagree with any form of animal experimentation or factory farming.)

However, in extreme circumstances, for example when people are starving, it is acceptable to eat food that is usually haram.

What are the implications of these rules for Muslims?

Obeying the food laws is all part of living a life that is pleasing to Allah. However, as with other laws that affect how a Muslim lives in a non-Muslim country, there are difficulties in keeping the rules:

- Some areas do not have halal butchers or shops that sell halal food.
- Some schools do not provide halal food for Muslim students.
- Many service stations on motorways do not have suitable food for Muslim travellers.
- Halal restaurants are quite difficult to find in some areas.

For discussion

In previous sections you have learned about taqwa – God-consciousness. How do you think obeying these laws on food helps a Muslim develop taqwa?

Summary

The Qur'an clearly sets out which foods are haram for a Muslim. Obeying the food laws is not a matter of choice but a clear part of being committed to Islam. Muslims believe that disobeying the laws, as with all haram acts, will lead to punishment in the life after death.

4.8 The implications of Muslim laws on riba and gambling when living in a capitalist society

Learning outcomes

By the end of this lesson, you should be able to:

- describe the laws on gambling and riba
- explain why these laws are important for Muslim society
- evaluate the importance of obeying these laws for a Muslim
- evaluate the effect of these laws for Muslims living in a non-Muslim society.

edexcel ▦ key terms

capitalism – The economic system adopted by most western governments.

riba – Any form of borrowing or lending money at interest.

Riba

Riba is charging interest on a loan. It is forbidden in Islam as it takes money from the poor and gives it to the rich. This is against all the principles of the ummah and zakah and can cause difficulties in a society that has an interest-based, **capitalist** economy.

Western banks work on the principle of lending money at interest to people who wish to buy houses or start businesses. The banks also have credit cards that allow people to buy things and pay for them over a period of time but with interest, so in all cases more is paid for the object than its original value. This means that the banks make money at the expense of the borrower, and this is forbidden in Islam.

In Islam, if someone is in need then it is the duty of the ummah to ensure that the need is met. If money is lent to another, then a reasonable time must be allowed for it to be paid back as well as no interest being charged. Part of being a community of believers is to share one's wealth and not exploit others or cause them to fall into more debt.

> 'If the debtor is in a difficulty, grant him time till it is easy for him to repay. But if you remit it by way of charity, that is best for you if you only knew.'
> (Surah 2:280)

Do you agree that this cartoon sums up Islamic attitudes to riba?

Muslim scholars have spent some time looking at these issues so that Allah's commands can be followed in a capitalist society. An example would be for Muslims to participate in one of the shared-equity schemes for house purchase, where a person buys a house in partnership with a bank or building society and gradually, through paying a set sum of money, each year owns more of the house. Many banks in the UK now offer Islamic bank accounts which do not involve interest.

Therefore, all forms of gambling – staking money on card games; horse racing; gambling machines; the lottery and so on – are forbidden in Islam.

For Muslims, winning something through gambling is the same as taking something illegally from another because you have not worked for it yourself.

> 'O you who believe! Intoxicants and gambling, (dedication of) stones, and (divination by) arrows, are an abomination – of Satan's handiwork: eschew such (abomination) that you may prosper. Satan's plan is (but) to incite enmity and hatred between you, with intoxicants and gambling, and hinder you from the remembrance of Allah and from prayer: will you not then abstain?' (Surah 5:93–94)

Activities

1 With a group of friends work out how much more you would pay if you borrowed £500 to buy a motorbike at 10% interest over three years.

2 Find out how Muslims manage to keep the laws on riba in the UK today. Do an Internet search or contact some local Muslims to help you.

What are the implications of these laws for Muslims?

• It can be difficult to buy property, yet renting often seems simply to make a landlord rich for not much work.
• If using a credit card, it should be paid off each month so that no interest is paid.
• Those with any spare money should give interest-free loans to anyone in need.
• Saving money should only be done in an ethically based investment.
• Money gained through exploitation of others should be given to charity.

Gambling

In Islam, Muslims are taught to follow Allah's commands for earning a living honestly through hard work and caring financially for the family and the community. Gambling makes a person dependent on chance or 'luck' and takes them away from serious work and productive effort.

Gambling wastes money that could be spent on the family.

Very few people win in gambling.

Allah has said nobody should have what they have not earned.

'Get rich quick' is against the spirit of Islam.

Gambling is addictive and can cause many problems for families and society.

Activities

3 Winning the lottery and giving away the money could help a lot of poor people. Prepare a short presentation explaining what might happen if a Muslim won a lot of money and gave it to the mosque. Give the arguments for and against using the money to help the poor.

Summary

Both riba and gambling are forbidden in the Qur'an as wealth gained without honest work is considered exploitation of other people. Money is a gift from Allah and must be used to benefit humanity.

4.9 How and why some Muslims are involved in working for social and community cohesion

Learning outcomes

By the end of this lesson, you should be able to:

- describe how some Muslims are involved in working for social and community cohesion
- explain why they are involved in this work
- evaluate the effect of this work on society in the UK.

Category	Numbers in the census
Christian	41,014,811
No religion	8,596,488
No answer	4,433,520
Muslim	1,588,890
Hindu	558,342
Sikh	336,179
Jewish	267,373
Other religions	159,167
Buddhist	149,157

UK population in the 2001 Census.

The copy of the 2001 census shows quite clearly that the UK is a multi-faith and multi-ethnic society, of which Muslims are a large part. Social and community cohesion is about helping all these different groups to live and work together in harmony. This also includes involving people of all ages and abilities.

A multi-faith, multi-ethnic society.

Why some Muslims work for social and community cohesion

- Muslims are taught in the Qur'an and by the example of the Prophet to be tolerant of the rights of others.
- The Qur'an teaches that there should be no compulsion in religion, so Muslims believe that all people should be free to practise what religion they choose.
- When Muhammad went to Medina and set up the first Muslim state, he established a constitution that included all the different groups – Jews, Pagan and Muslims – and ensured that each group had rights and responsibilities that contributed to the well-being of the whole society.

In the UK today there are many groups who work with all the religions and races in their area to establish good relationships. Their aim is to help all residents in a community, know each other and feel part of the community, and able to contribute regardless of age, religion, race, background, sex or profession.

With an increasing number of people entering the UK from other cultures around the world there is a greater need for people to feel welcome and part of the local community. Areas change as people move away and others move in, and so facilities, such as schools or specialist food shops, may be inadequate for a changing population.

Muslims believe that all humans are equal and created by Allah. This means that whether you are black or white, Muslim or non-Muslim, old or young, rich or poor, disabled or physically strong, you have a right to equal status in the community.

How some Muslims work for social and community cohesion

As the mosque is at the centre of the community, it is unsurprising that mosques are at the forefront of working for cohesion. A recent independent survey of mosques in the UK shows that:

Mosques contribute to their local communities through a wide range of services and activities in addition to providing space for worship, from sport and leisure activities to healthy living programs and assistance for senior citizens.

The survey charts how an overwhelming majority (94%) deliver educational programs for children and young people and three in five (61%) carry out women's groups/activities. It is also welcome information that increasingly more and more mosques have young people (52%) and women (15%) represented in their management responsibility. Far from being a source of separation, mosques are integral to community cohesion and development.

(Reported on the Muslim Media Network, from Charities Commission 2009)

Activities

1   Find out about any Muslim organisations that are working to develop social and community cohesion in your area. What work do they do?

Muslim bid for non-believers

A Muslim charity is bidding to run the first Islamic faith school for children who are not followers of the religion, The TES has learned.

The Al Habib Islamic Education and Cultural Centre said that 50 per cent of places at a new primary school, which serves a predominantly non-Muslim area, would be for local pupils.

Al Habib charity has put in a bid to run a 420-pupil primary school in Swindon, Wiltshire, due to be built at a cost of 7 million pounds. The charity says there is demand for the school from the Muslim community in the Swindon area. It is also claims there will be demand from non-Muslim families in the school's immediate catchment area. An hour of the timetable each day would be dedicated to studying Arabic and the Holy Quran. Non-Muslims pupils would be able to be exempted from the lessons, but it is hoped that the majority would choose to stay in class to gain more 'insight' into the Islamic faith.

(By David Marley, published in the *Times Educational Supplement* on 12 December 2008)

Activities

2   Read the article above very carefully. Do you think a school like this would work? Do you think it would help people in the community to feel part of one group? Make a list of things that the head teacher would have to consider when running such a school. How far would this school help community cohesion?

Summary

Muslims work for social and community cohesion because they believe that Allah created all human beings, and they follow the example of the Prophet who was prepared to work with different groups for the benefit of society.

4.10 How Muslim organisations help to relieve poverty in the UK

Learning outcomes

By the end of this lesson, you should be able to:

● describe the work of one Muslim organisation that is working to relieve poverty and suffering in the UK

● evaluate, with reasons, the effect of this work on society in the UK.

edexcel ⠿ key terms

sadaqah – Voluntary payment of charity or good acts of charity.

Poverty in the UK.

It is difficult to define poverty in the UK. In comparison with the developing world, very few people are starving or totally without shelter in the same way as they are in parts of Africa or Asia. However, many people who study how people live in the UK describe poverty as not having those things that are common in society, such as a good diet, warm and safe homes, and a job with a fair wage.

In the UK, the people most at risk of poverty are:

● those with low-paid jobs due to poor skills or lack of good education
● the unemployed
● the elderly
● refugees.

For many people in the UK, education and learning new skills helps them escape from the poverty trap. For the elderly, apart from specific organisations such as Age Concern, the government tries to help with various schemes – such as the winter fuel allowance.

However, many young people and families find themselves trapped in a situation where everyday living is a struggle. Muslims across the UK are trying to help, often through the local mosque.

Activities

1 There are a number of Muslim organisations that work to help the poor in the UK. Look at the Charity Commission's website (go to www.pearsonhotlinks.co.uk and enter express code 4264P) where you will be able to find a Muslim group near you. Find out what they do and the basis for their work. You need to research their work in the UK, *not* abroad.

ResultsPlus
Watch out!

This topic is specifically about organisations working in the UK – you must make sure you do not write about work that organisations carry out in other countries.

Muslim organisations working in the UK

One such organisation working towards the relief of poverty in the UK is the Husaini Islamic Centre in North London. What does it do?

1 It distributes zakah and **sadaqah** locally to support families of low income.

2 It helps widows and orphans financially.

3 It organises the collection of unwanted furniture and distributes it to those in need, free of charge.

4 It has a volunteer service that provides home help and respite through carers and visitors for the elderly who live alone and people who are ill at home or in hospital.

Another organisation is the Muslim Welfare House, based in Islington. A few of its aims, taken from its website, are:

• to improve the living conditions of the whole community in Islington, especially those groups who are marginalised

• to help people improve their quality of life through long-term, well-paid employment and self-employment

• to encourage young people to be part of the community by providing skills training and healthy lifestyle programmes.

In 2008 another organisation, the Scottish Islamic Association, organised a 'Qurbani' distribution. This used money raised at the end of Id to provide food and clothing for refugees in Glasgow.

Activities

2 Produce a wall display showing:

(a) why there is still a need for charities in the UK

(b) what one of these Islamic charities does to help

(c) how effective the work of the charity is.

For discussion

'It is the responsibility of the government, not individuals, to make sure no one is living in poverty.' Do you agree? Give reasons for your point of view.

Summary

There are still people living in poverty in the UK. Many Muslim groups work to try to relieve this poverty through financial aid and educational programmes.

4.11 The reasons why Muslim organisations work to relieve poverty and/or suffering in the UK

Learning outcomes

By the end of this lesson, you should be able to:

- explain the reasons why Muslims work to relieve poverty and suffering in the UK
- evaluate these reasons.

> A person who eats his fill while his neighbour remains hungry is not a believer.

For discussion

The Prophet Muhammad taught that a person should not let their neighbour go hungry while they have plenty to eat. What did he mean when he used the word 'neighbour'?

Why do Muslims help others?

All Muslim charities and organisations that help others do so for basically the same reasons:

1 Muslims believe that Allah has created everyone equal and therefore no one should be rich at the expense of others.

2 Care and compassion for others is part of showing one's love for Allah. Apart from zakah (see pages 64–65) Muslims are encouraged to give more to charity in the form of sadaqah. This is an individual making a gift in response to hearing about someone in need. If a Muslim hears about a problem and does nothing about it, that Muslim is ignoring the true meaning of ummah – community.

3 Faith in Allah is not just about belief but also about action. Muslims believe that Allah has given them everything they own and so they have a responsibility to ensure that what they have is used well, and that includes helping others. This is summed up in the Qur'an:

'... it is righteousness to believe in Allah and the Last Day, and the Angels, and the Book, and the Messengers; to spend of your substance, out of love for Him, for your kin, for orphans, for the needy, for the wayfarer, for those who ask, and for the ransom of slaves; to be steadfast in prayer, and practice regular charity.' (Surah 2:177)

Giving with the right intention will be rewarded by Allah.

How important is it for Muslims to help others?

- Obeying Allah is the most important thing for any Muslim, and Allah has commanded that they should give to charity and care for the needy.
- Muslims wish to become closer to Allah. Muhammad said that an ignorant person who is generous is closer to Allah than someone who is full of prayer but mean.
- Muslims believe that on the Last Day they will have to explain how they have used the gifts (especially wealth) that Allah has entrusted to them.
- Giving will be rewarded by Allah: *'Those who (in charity) spend of their goods by night and by day, in secret and in public, have their reward with their Lord…'* (Surah 2:274).
- Giving zakah purifies everything a Muslim owns.
- Islam is a brotherhood – ummah – and all Muslims should share with each other.
- Muhammad always helped other people in need and Muslims should follow his example.

Activities

1 Add to the wall display you started in Activity 2 on page 109 – the reasons why the organisation you have researched helps to relieve poverty and/or suffering in the UK.

ResultsPlus
Build Better Answers

Explain why **one** Muslim organisation helps to relieve poverty and/or suffering in the United Kingdom. (8 marks)

 Basic, 1–2-mark answers

Basic answers usually describe what the organisation does rather than give reasons why it does it.

 Good, 3–6-mark answers

Level two answers (3–4 marks) tend to give two reasons without any development. Level three answers (5–6 marks) will develop these reasons.

 Excellent, 7–8-mark answers

Most excellent answers will give four reasons. Other excellent answers will give fewer reasons but explain them. It is possible to get full marks by giving just one reason, but this would need to be explained in real depth.

Summary

Muslim organisations help to relieve suffering and/or poverty in the UK because they are following the command of Allah.

Quick quiz

1 What does 'halal' mean?

2 Give three examples of things that are haram.

3 What is the birth ceremony for Muslim babies called?

4 What happens to the body of a Muslim after death?

5 How should Muslim men and women dress?

6 What does 'riba' mean?

7 Give three reasons why gambling is haram.

8 What is meant by social and community cohesion?

9 Name one Muslim organisation that helps to relieve poverty and/or suffering in the UK.

10 Give three reasons why this organisation does this work.

Plenary activity

1 Draw idea maps or compile two tables – one of Islamic birth rituals and one of Islamic death rituals, explaining the meaning and significance of what happens during these rituals.

2 Complete the table below.

	Muslim laws	Problems in UK society?	How problems can be solved
Drugs and alcohol	Are haram	May cause problems with fitting in with non-Muslims in social situations	Many non-Muslims also do not drink alcohol or take drugs
Laws on dress			
Laws on food			
Laws on riba			
Laws on gambling			

Self-evaluation checklist

How well have you understood the topics in this section? In the first column of the table below use the following code to rate your understanding:

Green – I understand this fully.

Orange – I am confident I can answer most questions on this.

Red – I need to do a lot more work on this topic.

In the second and third columns you need to think about:

- whether you have an opinion on this topic and could give reasons for that opinion, if asked.
- whether you can give the opinion of someone who disagrees with you and give reasons for this alternative opinion.

Content covered	My understanding is red/orange/ green	Can I give my opinion?	Can I give an alternative opinion?
The meaning of halal and haram			
The significance of the concepts of halal and haram			
What is meant by greater jihad			
What is meant by lesser jihad			
How greater and lesser jihad effect a Muslim's life			
The meaning of Islamic birth rituals			
The significance of Islamic birth rituals			
The meaning of Islamic death rituals			
The significance of Islamic death rituals			
Muslim attitudes to drugs and alcohol			
Why these attitudes are important to a Muslim			
The implications of Muslim laws on dress when living in a western society			
The implications of Muslim laws on food when living in a western society			
The implications of Muslim laws on riba when living in a western society			
The implications of Muslim laws on gambling when living in a western society			
How some Muslims work for social and community cohesion			
Why some Muslims work for social and community cohesion			
How one Muslim organisation helps to relieve poverty and/or suffering in the UK			
The reasons why the organisation does this work			

KnowZone
Living the Muslim life

Introduction

In the exam you will see a choice of two questions on this module. Each question will include four tasks, which test your knowledge, understanding and evaluation of the material covered. A 2-mark question will ask you to define a term; a 4-mark question will ask your opinion on a point of view; an 8-mark question will ask you to explain a particular belief or idea; a 6-mark question will ask for your opinion on a point of view and ask you to consider an alternative point of view.

You must give your opinion, but must also include the reasons for your opinion. You need to give two reasons – any more than this and you will be wasting valuable time.

Mini exam paper

(a) What is **aqiqa**? (2 marks)

(b) Do you think religious dress laws are a good thing for Muslims today?

Give **two** reasons for your point of view. (4 marks)

(c) Explain how **one** Muslim organisation helps to relieve poverty and/or suffering in the United Kingdom. (8 marks)

(d) 'Islamic laws about riba do not work in a capitalist society.'

In your answer you should refer to Islam.

(i) Do you agree? Give reasons for your opinion. (3 marks)

(ii) Give reasons why some people may disagree with you. (3 marks)

Give a glossary definition. You do not need to write any more – often this can be done in one sentence.

This question is worth the most so it is important that you spend some time on it. 'Explain how' questions are asking you to connect two things and show how they are related to each other. In this case how the Muslim organisation connects to the relief of poverty and/or suffering. This is also the question where you should double-check the quality of your spelling and punctuation. Remember to take care when writing your answers, and to use proper sentences and not bullet points.

This question is always split into two parts and you should answer each part separately. For at least one of the parts you must refer to Muslim beliefs, and it's probably a good idea to consider what Muslims think first and then either use that for your own opinion or for the alternative opinion in (ii).

Mark scheme

(a) You will earn **2 marks** for a correct answer, and **1 mark** for a partially correct answer.

(b) To earn up to the full **4 marks** you need to give two reasons (as asked) and develop them. Two brief reasons or one developed reason will earn **2 marks** and one reason without development will earn **1 mark**.

(c) You can earn **7–8 marks** by giving up to four reasons, but the fewer reasons you give, the more you must develop them. You are being assessed on your use of language, so you also need to take care to express your understanding in a clear style of English and make some use of specialist vocabulary.

(d) To go beyond **3 marks** for the whole of this question you must refer to Islam. The more you are able to develop your reasons the more marks you will earn. Three simple reasons can earn you the same mark as one developed reason.

ResultsPlus
Build Better Answers

(d) 'Islamic laws about riba do not work in a capitalist society.'
   In your answer you should refer to Islam.
   (i) Do you agree? Give reasons for your opinion. (3 marks)
   (ii) Give reasons why some people may disagree with you. (3 marks)

Student answer	Comments	Improved student answer
(i) I agree because it is too difficult in the UK to keep when all the banks charge interest. (ii) Muslims would disagree because Allah's laws are perfect and will work everywhere. Also Muslims in the UK are managing to keep the law of riba.	The first statement in this answer is basic but correct, as the idea has not been developed or more than one reason given. Part two of the answer is better because two reasons have been given. Also the candidate has improved the answer by referring to Islam as the question asks.	(i) I agree because it is too difficult in the UK to keep riba when all the banks charge interest. This means Muslims would not be able to buy a house using a mortgage. The laws of riba are based on living in a society that keeps Shari'ah law so are not suitable for a capitalist society. (ii) Muslims would disagree because Allah's laws are perfect and will work everywhere. Also Muslims in the UK are managing to keep the law of riba by helping each other and lending money without interest. Also, by using special schemes where they share the cost of buying a property.

welcome to examzone

Revising for your exams can be a daunting prospect. In this part of the book we'll take you through the best way of revising for your exams, step by step, to ensure you perform as well as you can.

Zone In!

Have you ever become so absorbed in a task that suddenly it feels entirely natural and easy to perform? This is a feeling familiar to many athletes and performers. They work hard to recreate it in competition in order to do their very best. It's a feeling of being 'in the zone', and if you can achieve that same feeling in an examination, the chances are you'll perform brilliantly.

The good news is that you can get 'in the zone' by taking some simple steps in advance of the exam. Here are our top tips.

UNDERSTAND IT

Make sure you understand the exam process and what revision you need to do. This will give you confidence and also help you to get things into proportion. These pages are a good place to find some starting pointers for performing well in exams.

FRIENDS AND FAMILY

Make sure that your friends and family know when you want to revise. Even share your revision plan with them. Learn to control your times with them, so you don't get distracted. This means you can have better quality time with them when you aren't revising, because you aren't worrying about what you ought to be doing.

DEAL WITH DISTRACTIONS

Think about the issues in your life that may interfere with revision. Write them all down. Then think about how you can deal with each so they don't affect your revision.

COMPARTMENTALISE

You might not be able to deal with all the issues that can distract you. For example, you may be worried about a friend who is ill, or just be afraid of the exam. In this case, there is still a useful technique you can use. Put all of these worries into an imagined box in your mind at the start of your revision (or in the exam) and mentally lock it. Only open it again at the end of your revision session (or exam).

DIET AND EXERCISE

Make sure you eat sensibly and exercise as well! If your body is not in the right state, how can your mind be? A substantial breakfast will set you up for the day, and a light evening meal will keep your energy levels high.

BUILD CONFIDENCE

Use your revision time not only to revise content, but also to build your confidence in readiness for tackling the examination. For example, try tackling a short sequence of easy tasks in record time.

The key to success in exams and revision often lies in good planning. Knowing **what** you need to do and **when** you need to do it is your best path to a stress-free experience. Here are some top tips in creating a great personal revision plan.

First of all, *know your strengths and weaknesses.*

Go through each topic making a list of how well you think you know the topic. Use your mock examination results and/or any other test results that are available as a check on your self-assessment. This will help you to plan your personal revision effectively, putting extra time into your weaker areas.

Next, *create your plan!*

Remember to make time for considering how topics interrelate.

For example, in PE you will be expected to know not just about the various muscles, but how these relate to various body types.

The specification quite clearly states when you are expected to be able to link one topic to another so plan this into your revision sessions.

Finally, *follow the plan!*

You can use the revision sections in the following pages to kick-start your revision.

MAY

SUNDAY	MONDAY	TUES
29	30	1

Be realistic about how much time you can devote to your revision, but also make sure you put in enough time. Give yourself regular breaks or different activities to give your life some variance. Revision need not be a prison sentence!

Find out your exam dates. Go to the Edexcel website **www.edexcel.com** to find all final exam dates, and check with your teacher.

view Secti
complete t
ractice ex
question

7

8

Chunk your revision in each subject down into smaller sections. This will make it more manageable and less daunting.

Draw up a list of all the dates from the start of your revision right through to your exams.

13

Review Sectio
Complete three
practice exam

20

Review Sectio
Try the Keyter
Quiz again

Make sure you allow time for assessing your progress against your initial self-assessment. Measuring progress will allow you to see and be encouraged by your improvement. These little victories will build your confidence.

22

EXAM DAY!

27

28

29

As you get close to completing your revision, the Big Day will be getting nearer and nearer. Many students find this the most stressful time and tend to go into panic mode, either working long hours without really giving their brains a chance to absorb information, or giving up and staring blankly at the wall.

Panicking simply makes your brain seize up and you find that information and thoughts simply cannot flow naturally. You become distracted and anxious, and things seem worse than they are. Many students build the exams up into more than they are. Remember: the exams are not trying to catch you out! If you have studied the course, there will be no surprises on the exam paper!

Student tips

I know how silly it is to panic, especially if you've done the work and know your stuff. I was asked by a teacher to produce a report on a project I'd done, and I panicked so much I spent the whole afternoon crying and worrying. I asked other people for help, but they were panicking too. In the end, I calmed down and looked at the task again. It turned out to be quite straightforward and, in the end, I got my report finished first and it was the best of them all!

In the exam you don't have much time, so you can't waste it by panicking. The best way to control panic is simply to do what you have to do. Think carefully for a few minutes, then start writing and as you do, the panic will drain away.

Don't panic

If you are sitting your exams from 2014 onwards, you will be sitting all your exams together at the end of your course. Make sure you know in which order you are sitting the exams, and prepare for each accordingly - check with your teacher if you're not sure. They are likely to be about a week apart, so make sure you allow plenty of revision time for each before your first exam.

You will have one and a half hours for this exam paper and in that time you have to answer **four** questions, one on each of the four sections you have studied: Beliefs and values, Community and tradition, Worship and celebration, Living the Muslim life.

In each section, you can make a choice from two questions.

Each question will be made up of four different parts:

- a 2-mark question will ask for you to define a term
- a 4-mark question will ask for your opinion on a point of view
- an 8-mark question will ask you to explain a particular belief or idea
- a 6-mark question will ask for your opinion on a point of view and ask you to consider an alternative point of view.

Effectively you shouldn't spend more than 22.5 minutes on each section (that's 90 minutes divided by 4):

- the 8-mark question deserves the most attention, so that's around 9 minutes
- the 2-mark question should take you 1.5 minutes, then
- 5 minutes for the 4-mark question, and
- the remaining 7 minutes for the 6-mark question.

Obviously you can give or take here or there, and your teacher may guide you differently, but as long as you don't go over 22.5 minutes altogether and the length of each of your answers is appropriate for the number of marks available, then you'll be on the right lines.

Meet the exam paper

This diagram shows the front cover of the exam paper. These instructions, information and advice will always appear on the front of the paper. It is worth reading it carefully now. Check you understand it. Now is a good opportunity to ask your teacher about anything you are not sure of here.

Print your surname here, and your other names afterwards to ensure that the exam board awards the marks to the right candidate.

Here you fill in the school's exam number.

Ensure that you understand exactly how long the examination will last, and plan your time accordingly.

Note that the quality of your written communication will also be marked. On the questions with an asterisk (*) take particular care to present your thoughts and work at the highest standard you can.

Here you fill in your personal exam number. Take care when writing it down because the number is important to the exam board when writing your score.

In this box, the examiner will write the total marks you have achieved in the exam paper.

Make sure that you understand exactly which questions from which sections you should attempt.

Don't feel that you have to fill the answer space provided. Everybody's handwriting varies, so a long answer from you may take up as much space as a short answer from someone else.

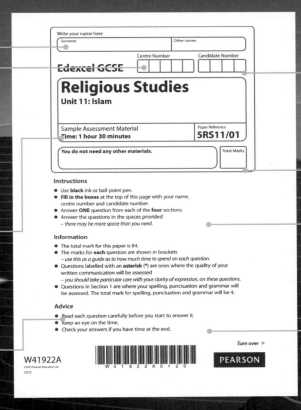

Practical tips on the exam paper

- You must use a black pen. Your paper is scanned into a computer for marking. If you write in any other colour, you risk your work not being seen clearly.

- You must choose your question carefully – cross out the one you are not going to do – to avoid changing a question half-way through answering it. This is a very common mistake and costs candidates lots of marks!

- Mark with an x at the top of the page which question you have chosen.

- Do not write outside the guidelines – your answer may get cut off by the scanning process.

- Do not use extra sheets and attach them unless it is absolutely necessary. If you need more space – for example, for a (b) question – continue into the (c) space and when you change question write your own (c). Do the same for (c) into (d). If you then run out, put an arrow and write at the end of the exam booklet.

This section provides answers to the most common questions students have about what happens after they complete their exams. For more information, visit www.pearsonhotlinks.co.uk (express code 4264P) and click on 'ExamZone'.

About your grades

Whether you've done better than, worse than, or just as you expected, your grades are the final measure of your performance on your course and in the exams. On this page we explain some of the information that appears on your results slip and tell you what to do if you think something is wrong. We answer the most popular questions about grades and look at some of the options facing you.

When will my results be published?

Results for summer examinations are issued on the third Thursday in August. January exam results are issued in March and March exam results are issued in April. If you are sitting your exams from 2014 onwards, there will no longer be January sittings: you will sit all of your exams in June.

Can I get my results online?

Visit www.pearsonhotlinks.co.uk (express code 4264P) and click on 'Results Plus', where you will find detailed student results information including the 'Edexcel Gradeometer' which demonstrates how close you were to the nearest grade boundary.

I haven't done as well as I expected. What can I do now?

First of all, talk to your subject teacher. After all the teaching, tests and internal examinations that you have had, he/she is the person who best knows what grade you are capable of achieving. Take your results slip to your subject teacher, and go through the information on it in detail. If you both think there is something wrong with the result, the school or college can apply to see your completed examination paper and then, if necessary, ask for a re-mark immediately. Bear in mind that the original mark can be confirmed or lowered, as well as raised, as a result of a re-mark.

How do my grades compare with those of everybody else who sat this exam?

You can compare your results with those of others in the UK who have completed the same examination using the information on the Edexcel website accessed at www.pearsonschoolsandfecolleges.co.uk/hotlinks (express code 4264P) by clicking on 'Edexcel'.

What happens if I was ill over the period of my examinations?

If you become ill before or during the examination period you are eligible for special consideration. This also applies if you have been affected by an accident, bereavement or serious disturbance during an examination.

If my school has requested special consideration for me, is this shown on my Statement of Results?

If your school has requested special consideration for you, it is not shown on your results slip, but it will be shown on a subject mark report that is sent to your school or college. If you want to know whether special consideration was requested for you, you should ask your Examinations Officer.

Can I have a re-mark of my examination paper?

Yes, this is possible, but remember that only your school or college can apply for a re-mark, not you or your parents/carers. First of all, you should consider carefully whether or not to ask your school or college to make a request for a re-mark. It is worth knowing that very few re-marks result in a change to a grade – not because Edexcel is embarrassed that a change of marks has been made, but simply because a re-mark request has shown that the original marking was accurate. Check the closing date for re-marking requests with your Examinations Officer.

When I asked for a re-mark of my paper, my subject grade went down. What can I do?

There is no guarantee that your grades will go up if your papers are re-marked. They can also go down or stay the same. After a re-mark, the only way to improve your grade is to take the examination again. Your school or college Examinations Officer can tell you when you can do that.

Can I resit this unit?

If you are sitting your exams before 2014, you may resit a unit once prior to claiming certification for the qualification. If you are sitting your exams from 2014 onwards, you will not be able to resit any of the exams.

For much more information, go to www.pearsonhotlinks.co.uk (express code 4264P) and click on 'ExamZone'.

Glossary

This is an extended glossary containing definitions that will help you in your studies. Edexcel key terms are not included as all of these are defined in the lessons themselves.

adhan – The call to prayer.

akhirah – Muslim beliefs about life after death.

Allah – Arabic word for 'God'.

barzakh – The time between death and the Last Day.

burka – Outer garment worn by women in some Islamic traditions which cloaks the entire body.

calligraphy – Artistic handwriting: associated with Islam, most often used for copying the Qur'an; script, throughout many languages including Arabic. Calligraphy was the primary means for the preservation of the Qur'an.

CE – Common era.

Ghadir e Khum – Place where Muhammad delivered a sermon after his final hajj.

hafiz – Someone who can recite the Qur'an from memory.

idolatry – Worshipping anything, or any other being than Allah.

ihram – State of purity. Also the name of the clothing worn by pilgrims.

injil – Allah's revelation to Isa (Jesus). Some scholars equate this to the four Gospels of the Christian Bible.

intercession – The idea that Muhammad can pass prayers on to Allah.

iqamah – The command to rise and worship Allah.

Isa – **Muslim** name for Jesus.

Jahannam – Hell.

Ka'bah – The most sacred site to Muslims, located at Makkah.

khutbah – A sermon, or formal public teaching on the Qur'an.

Makkah – Birthplace of Muhammad, the most important holy place in Islam and destination for Muslims on hajj.

makruh – A disliked or offensive act: not something that is haram (forbidden), so not a sin, nevertheless abstaining from a makruh act is pleasing to Allah.

mosque – A building where Muslims can go to pray.

Muttaqi – A truly obedient Muslim.

Night of Power – The most important event in the life of Muhammad, when he received the words of Allah from the Angel Jibril (Gabriel) for the first time.

niqab – Veil.

niyyah – Intention.

sin – An act contrary to the will of Allah.

Sufi – Group of Muslims who emphasise the spiritual rather than the physical aspects of Islam, especially closeness to Allah, and frequently use music and dance to demonstrate this.

surah – A chapter of the Qur'an.

talbiyah – The words of Ibrahim (Abraham) which show that the pilgrim is waiting and ready for Allah.

taqwa – God-consciousness.

tawrat – The prophecy given by Allah to the prophet Musa (Moses), sometimes equated to the Jewish Torah or the five Books of Moses from the Christian Bible.

tasbih – Prayer beads.

zabur – Collection of hymns and songs which Muslims believe were written by Dawud (David). Some scholars equate this to the Biblical book of Psalms.

Index

Key terms from the beginning of each topic are shown as main entries in bold type, and the page number that is also in bold will take you to a definition of the word.

A

abortion 50
Abraham *see* Ibrahim
Adam 12, 13, 19, 78
Aga Khan 51
Ahmadiyya 51
akhirah 24–25, 97
al-Qadar 14, 14–15
alcohol 98–99
Allah
    creativity 8, 8–9
    forgiveness of 69, 71, 77–79, 81
    names of 10–11, 35
    oneness 4–5, 61
    qualities of 10–11, 60
    submission to 14
angels 16–17
    see also Jibril
aqiqa 94
Arabic 4, 33, 34, 41, 44–45, 50, 62, 74
Arafat 78, 75, 78–79, 81
authority 34, 13, 32, 34–35, 39

B

Barelvi 51
barzakh 24–25
birth 94–95
    see also **aqiqa**
bismillah 34, 10–11
burqa 100, 101

C

Caliphs 48–49
calligraphy 36
capitalism 104, 91
    and **riba** and gambling 104–105
charity *see* **sadaqah**; **zakah**
children *see* **aqiqa**
Christianity 6, 19–21, 89, 101, 106
circumcision *see* khitan
communication 16–19, 62

community 46–47, 106–107
    see also **ummah**
creativity 8, 8–9, 77, 79
culture 40–41, 50–51, 74
    multiculturalism 41, 89, 100, 107

D

dance 51–53
Dar-ul-Islam 90, 90–91
Day of Judgement 15, 17, 24, 25, 49,
    78–79, 96, 98
death *see* **janazah**
din 4, 4–5
Deobandi 51
dress 50, 72, 74, 76, 82, 100–101
    uniform 60
drugs 98–99

E

education 45, 61, 82, 94, 108–109

F

faith *see* **iman**
fasting 39, 68–73, 75
Five Pillars 25, 49, 53, 59–60, 93
    see also **hajj**; **salah**; **sawm**;
        Shahadah; **zakah**
food laws *see* **halal**
free will 14–15
funerals *see* **janazah prayers**

G

gambling 104–105
Gates, Bill 64
gender 3, 43, 50, 72, 74, 76, 89, 100–101
Ghadir e Khum 50
greater jihad 92, 7, 92–93

H

hadith 32, 32–33, 39, 53, 69, 98
hafiz 3
hajj 74, 41, 59, 74–83, 97
    described 74–75

difficulty of 83
meaning of 76
significance of 77
see also **Arafat**; **Id-ul-Adha**;
    Makkah; Mina
halal 90, 45, 82, 89, 90–91, 102–103
haram 90, 25, 45, 90–91, 93, 99,
    102–103
hijab 100, 74, 100–101
    see also dress
holy books 20–21
    see also **Qur'an**

I

ibadah 6, 25, 61, 68, 70, 73, 103
Ibrahim 19, 76, 78, 81–83
Id-ul-Adha 82, 75, 81, 83
Id-ul-Fitr 72, 72–73
idolatry 5, 6–7, 60
    of angels 17
    see also **shirk**
ihram 74–75, 82, 97
imam 44, 44–45, 57, 51, 97
    Sunni and **Shi'ah** 49
iman 8
injil 20–21
intercession 51
Islam 4
Isa (Jesus) 6, 19–21
Ithnasheri 51

J

Jahannam 24
Jamaatkhana 51
janazah prayers 96, 97
Jesus *see* Isa
Jibril 22, 23, 69
jihad 7
    greater jihad 92, 7, 92–93
    lesser jihad 92
Judaism 19–21, 101, 106

K

Ka'bah 6, 7, 41, 43, 76–78
Karbala 49
khalifah 12, 12–13, 48–49
khitan (circumcision) 94

L

language *see* Arabic
law 39, 45
　　see also **Shari'ah**
lesser jihad 92
life after death *see* akirah

M

Madinah 49
madrasah 94, 46–47, 90, 92, 94, 95
masjid 42
Makkah 6, 32, 41–43, 49, 74–77, 81, 83, 97
　　facing in prayer 62
　　number of visitors to 59
　　see also **hajj**
makruh 90
McDonald's 92
Mina 75, 78, 80–81
Moses *see* Musa
mosques
　　in the UK 31, 46, 50–51, 73, 89, 100
　　domes, symbolism of 8, 43
　　features of 42–43
　　first 42
　　see also **imam**
Muhammad
　　death of 48–49
　　example of 5, 6, 91, 111
　　as intercessor 51
　　life of 32, 61, 69, 76–78
　　as Seal of the Prophets 19, 32–33, 61
　　Qur'an revealed to 14, 16–17, 21, 22–23, 32–33, 35, 36, 61, 74, 76
multiculturalism 41, 89, 91, 100, 107
Musa (Moses) 19–21
music 51–53
Muslim 4
Muttaqi 71
Muzdalifah 81

N

Najaf 49
Night of Power 22–23, 33, 69
number of Muslims worldwide 59

P

poverty 66–67, 108–111
　　see also **zakah**
prayer 15, 16, 40, 41, 62–63
　　at **Arafat** 79
　　in a mosque 42–45
　　see also **salah**
prison 45, 65
prophets 18–21, 23, 33, 35
　　see also Muhammad

Q

qadi 38, 39
qiblah 76, 41, 43, 76, 97
Qur'an 4
　　authority of 34–35
　　described 34
　　importance of 3
　　respect for 36–37
　　revealed to Muhammad 14, 16–17, 21, 22–23, 32–33, 35, 36, 61, 74, 76

R

race 40–41, 66, 74, 82, 106
Ramadan 68, 68–73
responsibility 12–13
riba 104, 104–105
risalah 18, 18–19

S

sacrifice 81, 82–83
sadaqah 108, 65, 108–109, 110
salah 62, 41, 44, 49, 51, 59–63, 70, 77, 81, 90
　　forgetting 69
　　at funerals 86
　　importance of 63
sanctity of life 5, 9, 13, 50, 66
Satan 71, 81, 103
sawm 68, 63, 68–69, 71, 81
school *see* education
science 8–9
Seal of the Prophets 19, 32–33, 61

sermons 44, 78
Shahadah 60, 6, 23, 49, 60–61
Shari'ah 38, 25, 38–39, 45, 53, 90–91, 93, 98
Shi'ah 48, 48–51
　　Ithnasheri 51
shirk 6, 6–7, 33, 53
Sikhism 89, 106
Sin 6–7, 25, 33, 49, 77, 96, 99
　　forgiveness of 69, 71, 77–79, 81
　　see also **shirk**
stoning 75–76, 80–81
sufism 51, 52–53
sunnah 32, 32–33, 39, 94–95, 98
Sunni 48, 48–51
　　Barelvi 51
　　Deobandi 51

T

taqwa 25, 65, 69, 71, 103
tasbih 11
tawaf 76, 75–76
tawhid 4, 4–5, 41
tawrat 20–22
Topkapi Palace 4

U

UK, Islam in the 31, 46, 50–51, 73, 89, 100
ulama 38, 39
ummah 40, 40–41, 45, 47, 94–95, 104, 110, 111
　　and fasting 70, 71 77
　　and festivals 73, 74, 82–83
　　and **tawaf** 76
　　and **zakah** 66–67

W

westernisation 45
　　and capitalism 104–105
　　and dress 50, 100–101
　　and food laws 102–103
whirling dervishes 52
women *see* gender
wudu 62, 37, 62

Z

zabur 20–21
zakah 64, 41, 49, 63, 64–67, 69, 105, 109, 110, 111